LIFE
Doesn't Have to be
PERFECT
to be Wonderful

---

this way is my way

LIFE
Doesn't Have to be
PERFECT
to be Wonderful

this way is my way

Richard Todd
CANTON

LIFE DOESN'T HAVE TO BE PERFECT TO BE WONDERFUL
THIS WAY IS MY WAY

iUniverse books may be ordered through booksellers or by contacting:

iUniverse
1663 Liberty Drive
Bloomington, IN 47403
www.iuniverse.com
1-800-Authors (1-800-288-4677)

ISBN: 978-1-4917-7583-7 (sc)
ISBN: 978-1-4917-7582-0 (hc)
ISBN: 978-1-4917-7581-3 (e)

Library of Congress Control Number: 2015914070

Print information available on the last page.

iUniverse rev. date: 08/28/2015

This book is dedicated to the kind and gentle people of Truro, Nova Scotia starting with Mayor William (Bill) R. Mills. As I faced the biggest challenge of my adult life, these people rose in my defense and embraced me in such a way that I felt I truly belonged. It is with sincere thanks that I acknowledge these people who have shown compassion, kindness and support on so many levels that I suspect I will call this place home for a long time to come.

Truro, established in 1875 has a lot going for it starting with her people. There is exists approximately 12,500 citizens and up to 17,000 if you include surrounding areas. We lay claim to the beautiful and spacious Victoria Park, the hundred year old Nova Scotia Agriculture College/ Dalhousie Campus, some impressive wooden statues, and the best flooding in the country thanks to the Salmon River but there exists here a true sense of community and it has produced some citizens worth mentioning. Brett Lauther CFL player, Portia White, singer, Drew Bezanson, bike enthusiast, Jana Miller, vocalist, Zack Sill, hockey player, Mercedes Blair, nature photographer, Su Burnett, Animal Whisperer, Nora Bernard, Activist, Pencil artist extraordinaire Robb Scott, Robert Stanfield, politician, Humanitarian Tracey Dorrington-Skinner and so many more that there isn't enough room to mention. (Okay a few.. actors. the Trailer Park Boys, Ben Arnfast, Wayne Burns and Eric what's his name, the golfer,)

Let me put it this way, there are so many interesting and talented people in this town that there's no telling who can accomplish what, the question is when.

This book is a collection of inspirational stories and events that have shaped my adult life and my attitude toward it I have come to the major conclusion that no matter what you are facing, giving up is not an option.

Due to circumstances beyond my immediate control, I have had to face some things that have knocked me down but for some reason couldn't keep me there. With the love and support of family and friends, I was able to pick myself up, dust myself off and keep marching. I believe that you can too!

I hope you find a blessing amongst the pages.

It's Great Being Todd!

I am Richard Todd Canton, Todd to friends and family, Canton to the young persons who knew me from school and Stupid to my ex-wife, he he.

I have to tell you I am a happy man. I am certainly a lucky man but mostly I am a man who is blessed. I am also smart enough to realize all of this and to be truly grateful for all I have and pay little attention to what I don't have.

I was born smack dab in the middle of a lovely family and grew up in a picturesque neighborhood. I breathed in fresh air and drank clean water. Summers were filled eating wild blueberries, climbing dog-berry trees and riding my bike across the vast marshes that surrounded our town. Every day was an adventure whether I realized it or not at the time. I learned to love nature but more than that I learned to respect it.

In my early years I formed a great love for the animal kingdom and it has continued throughout my life. I was taught to enjoy a sunset from our front lawn and told that at one time the same sky was filled with the smoke of war and that despite any losses then we all won in the long run.

I learned the true meaning of love in the arms of my mother and father and in the embrace of my siblings, one brother and five sisters, all of whom I hold in high regard. At this age all our childish and immature squabbles are a thing of the past and maybe, just maybe at fifty I have finally grown up. My mother said it would happen one day.

I have some of the most wonderful and interesting friends any man could ask for. I have those were there when I needed them and more that wished they were. That's good enough to me. During my journey I have had the honor of being asked to be a god-father to some amazing individuals. First my niece Sara whom I think of as my own daughter, to Jenna, Jaden and Julissa McIntyre and Kayla MacLellan. I was even the man of honor at my friend Annette's wedding.

I was privileged to be married to the only person I will ever truly love and as a result have remained a solitary man since our breakup at 28 years. Ouch my heart. If I could undo anything I think I might just pull my selfish head out of my ass and take a second look at the decisions I made and didn't make, but should have.

I suffered devastating blows in losing family members and friends to death that should never have happened when they did, starting with my father when I was eleven years old. It left me lonely and sad as a boy and lost as an adolescent. However with the help of an understanding and tolerant mother, I made it. Having so many sisters to influence and spoil me I am to say the least, sensitive.

I was taught at an early age to take every negative thing in my life and turn it into something positive. I do that same thing today but once a while I get discouraged and want to throw in the towel ..though I never do it. My mother and her people, the resilient coal mining kind, taught me to never give up, no matter what. And no matter what *has* happened to me. I have survived having my life turned upside down and shaken with sex charges stemming from my working as a teacher's assistant. Not really sure how I got thru that one but here I am and I am still standing.

I watched my sister who unexpectedly became a widow battle breast cancer like a trooper and she got thru that. All we could do as a family is support her. In fact those of us who found our way into our mother's clutch has had our fair share of crap to face and yet we all seem to get through it all. I think we get a lot of this from her, our mother. A maverick of epic proportion, she, a widow at 43 showed us the way to go. In the end it was up to each and every one of us to decide if what she taught sank in. For some it did and others, not so much.

I am a strong, stubborn and mule headed person but I can be reached. I do not respond well to screaming or hollering and for heaven's sake, do not talk down to me. I am a diligent and competent worker and I hope to work until the day comes when I can do so no longer. I have dabbled in a few different careers but food service is first, last and always in the forefront of what I do best. I am a decent cook but I am much better at eating.

As much as I love eating, I love music. Not a big fan of TV I would rather have music playing in the background. I don't even have to mention anyone other than my favorite singer Anne Murray to explain that I am a fan of flawless melodies and rich voices that sing not only to my ears but straight to my heart.

I am a competitive person but mostly with myself constantly trying to outdo my last accomplishment.

I possess a great sense of humor and I believe I have good comedic timing. But let's be honest, not everyone finds me hilarious. I think if a person takes themselves too seriously they will seriously drive themselves and those around them nuts. However, take your craft seriously and it will seriously serve you well. A good work ethic and a good ethic for life are two very important virtues for any man, woman or child.

I have never intentionally harmed another human being and I am a firm believer in life, liberty and the pursuit of happiness. Take a chance and see what happens. If you fall, learn from that. If you rise, learn from that too! I encourage everyone I meet and I learn something from every single one of them, how to or how not to act. I take the things I have learned and put them in story form and present them to the world. As a result, I have received some serious responses both positive and negative. I prefer the positive ones.

I am happy with who I am and despite any shortcomings, I am a good man. I have gotten knocked down more than once but I always get up again. I have been both a hero and a victim. I am more than all that, I am a happy man.

It really is great being Todd!

Life Doesn't Have to be Perfect to be Wonderful!

Now where do I begin? Well wherever it is I must remember to save my data, I lost a lot due to my own negligence as I am technically declined. However, it made me rethink what I had to say. I hope this is much more interesting. Whatever it is or where it comes from I am setting out to prove that life is really worth living no matter where you are or what you have been through. We have to learn to *live in moments rather than time* and to cherish these moments because in life we have to face a lot and some of it is not very nice. I do believe that we can get through anything as long as you surround yourself with supportive people and that anything can be handled one day at a time. Just sayin'....

I am a working man. In the last ten years I have worked as a waiter, a store clerk, a television host, an author, a newspaper column writer, and a teacher's assistant and that was all at the same time. I have made a pretty good name for myself by being genuine and kind in business and in life. So you can imagine when my world was turned upside down by an accusation from a student in junior high, just how surprised I was when the whole town rose in my defense, embraced me and supported me. I looked into the lens of a TV camera and stated that I had stood up for every kid in this town and I hope someone will stand up for me and *by God above* the whole town did, save one or two. I am humbled by the love and generosity sent my way and as a result I am stronger and more determined than ever to reach out to people with a kind and generous heart.

Richard Todd Canton

If I am not willing to allow anything to keep me down, then how about you?

Here's one of the most important things I have learned. Never give in to labels nor opinion, be your own person.

Never Give up on Yourself as

Others will Surely Follow!

I am a firm believer in the human race. Oh don't get me wrong, I have been let down on quite a few occasions but yet I cannot quite give up on mankind quite yet. I do not want them to give up on me either.

I have had my heart bruised by acts of violence against animals. I have witnessed selfish acts and some unselfish ones that continue to restore my faith in humanity. I have seen animal rescues, people pulled from burning vehicles and homes, fireman and police risking their own lives to save others and ordinary citizens performing acts of bravery that should never go unheralded.

Yet we continue to place Hollywood stars on pedestals. I agree with it but only if I see the good they have done with their fame and fortune. I consider it a responsibility for all successful and rich people to share the wealth be it monetary or their time. It is called giving back and I feel it sets a good example to us all.

I think everyone should be kind to young children and old people but why not kind to everyone? I especially think people should respect the animal kingdom. I like most people I meet but I sure hate those who perform unspeakable crimes against others in and out of the animal kingdom and I despise even more those who don't speak up. Stand up against them.

So here comes the advice. If you don't want a cat don't take home a kitten, same as a dog. Don't have kids if you don't want teenager saround because before you know it they are fully grown.

I feel that I am hopelessly romantic and I truly believe that love conquers all and that hate is is poison and it easily overtakes people. So don't get caught up in it. If you feel the people in your circle are bringing you down, get a new circle. It is just as easy to love as it is to hate.

Surround yourself by those who acknowledge and support you, it makes a world of difference.

Never give up on yourself or others will surely follow.

I am your server Todd, I am happy to do so.....but........don't push it!

Growing up in the food business like I did means an awful lot to me and makes up a huge chunk of who I am today. First of all, I am no stranger to hard work. I started out in a restaurant kitchen as a dishwasher, then a cook's assistant, a cook itself and then a server. It is in serving the public that I have found my true calling and where I am the most at home. I believe that I have the right type of personality to deal with the public. I feel that I am an easy going and humorous individual, and I treat my guest like guests, but don't push it.

A server is a very busy person with a lot on their mind. We are champions at multi-tasking. Most of us are friendly but some are not. We are knowledgeable and insightful. We are also tolerant and understanding where our guests are concerned. We can give directions, make suggestions, predict the weather, and even call a hockey game. We do all of this with a smile on our faces, but don't push it.

As a conscientious server I see the guests as just that, guests. I save all my best behavior and abilities for them. It is after all the guests that I work for not necessarily the restaurant. I have a petty good reputation in the food business and a good customer following. So if need be, I take them with me wherever I go.

Hot fresh food served in a clean friendly environment. Having said that, don't push it.

Servers are generally knowledgeable people with great skills for interacting with even the most difficult of people. Don't try to banter with a server because we have become experts at it. Well, go ahead but do so only if you are the type that can dish it out and can take it too.

Never assume that you know what we are going through or that you know how we are feeling. We, the servers are able to hide our broken hearts, our troubled personal lives and our drama. At least those of us worth our salt are able to. We can hold everything inside and put on a very brave face for the public, but don't push it.

Don't assume servers are working in this profession until something better comes along. Some of us are in it for the long haul.

We know our menu and we can answer just about any question. We know what's good, what is the best seller, what gets the most complaints and just about everything else, so ask us. A good server will guide you, a great one will tell you exactly where to go.

Servers like it when the public is on the ball. Guests quite often have coupons, gift cards and angles. Some are genuine and others want something for nothing. Never assume that the server cannot read the fine print on a coupon because they have already had twenty-seven of them this week alone. So talk to and check with them and everything will run smoothly.

Don't ever ask a server about tips. First of all it is none of your business and it really is personal. Don't push it!

Servers enjoy the company of regular customers but not complacent ones. We love it when our guest knows what they want and we soon become familiar with those we can make suggestions to and those we can not. We have had our fair share of whiners, grumblers and those that just plain nasty. We are up for the challenge. The kind and elderly make up for any of the challenging ones. We can handle them all, but don't push it.

The server hears everything you say and everything else that is said at the table despite the fact that we are not looking directly into your face at the time. Please be aware that we hear every comment whether it is positive or negative. People do not realize that they might be talking about something delicate and just who is hearing it. Now don't get me wrong, most of us are discrete and allow it to roll off but others are curious to hear more. We can also hear you as we walk away. It's our loaded gun, it decides whether or not you are classed as a difficult table or not. So don't push it!

Here's your job as a guest. Make yourself comfortable and scan the menu. I, as the server will take your drink order while you decide what to eat. Seniors like tea and the hotter the better. One teabag can take about four pots of hot water, did you know that? Pop goes great with burgers, fries and such. I will keep your glass full. Then are are those who only drink water. Water comes in many forms in a restaurant and has many names. There is bottled water, sparkling water and flavoured water. Then there is good old tap water also known as 'just water', H2O, water on the rocks, Adam's Ale, water with ice, straight up water, lemon water, water for now, the clear stuff and just plain water.

Don't ever get me wrong where my guests are concerned. I love my job and I have cultivated a considerable collection of loyal customers and I appreciate every single one of them. If I do come across a tough nut or two I personally challenge myself to win them over.

Sometimes I do, sometimes I don't, such is life.

Death becomes you

Maybe it's just me but I am sure that an awful lot of good people have passed away and some of them meant a lot to me. I am no stranger to grief. After losing my parents I can safely say nothing hurts as much. No, I take that back, losing a pet can be just as devastating as anything else.

Death is something I fear. My father died when I was a little boy. It seemed to me that he missed a lot over the years. I don't want that to happen to me I was devastated by him leaving us.

I am a lucky man, I have escaped death on a few occasions and it has made me very grateful. What a waste to die at any age and leave a life un-lived. That in itself is the real shame.

If you allow grief to take over you that is exactly what it will do, take over. Grieving is a part of life just like happiness, sadness, the blues. They are all human emotions and most are felt on a daily basis. That's okay! Fight them, if you allow a certain emotion take over it wins and you unfortunately, lose. I think you get what I am saying. Don't let death become you.

If you wallow in sadness and pity you will find that your friends will head for the hills and you will find it increasingly difficult to find a sympathetic ear. As a boy suffering the loss of my father, it sent me into a deep depression. I longed for answers and for some justice. I turned naturally to my surviving parent for comfort. Thank God that woman was there. This is what she taught me. Take all your emotions, the sadness, loss and grief and put them into an imaginary photo album, close it and place it on a high shelf, out of the way. Then, once in a while, take it down, open it up and feel all those emotions but when you are done, close the book and put it back on that high shelf until the next time. Pretty smart eh?

My Mother was the smartest woman I have ever met, and I am not saying that because she was my mother because I have a lot of dumb sisters. Just sayin'.

So the moral to this story: Become accepting of the things you cannot change (like death), embrace the memories, the good and bad ones, and keep marching. Their troubles are over, yours continue on. Make the most of the moments of your your life as they are quickly gone.

God bless us all.

Spenny

I will do anything for the People I Love, but I won't do anything for those I don't!

Now, some people might take that statement one way and others, another. What it means is that I am a loyal fellow. When I love someone or something, I commit. So that leaves little for all the rest. I tend to be an over achiever in nearly everything I do. This has proven to be both a help and a hindrance.

For instance, I love my friend Spencer, he is kinda like a son to me. I probably would do anything for him. He is someone I met when he came to our restaurant to work after just turning sixteen. I liked him right away. Since I have no children of my own I can only imagine what a child of mine would be like. He is the one who comes to mind when I think of what God might have given me in the form of a son. His birthday is the day before mine therefore we share the same astrological sign. We also share some similar traits. Both of us have a stubborn streak a mile long, don't respond well to criticism, and lean toward a healthy soul, mind and body. Music is up there on the list, food too. Having said all of this, he is, in many ways, a 'mini me'. He might disagree, for that matter, me too!

At first Spencer was this genuinely nice kid, kind and considerate. But, as these things go......it seems that Spencer is independent, head strong and determined. He is also emotional, naive and gullible. He makes mistakes. I felt from the first day we met that on some cosmic level, he needed me. After all I am the voice of reason. Now if someone else was telling the story it might go like this. *Todd has no children of his own so he finds needy people and they fill a void.* It could be true. Or maybe he needs someone like me who sees him heading toward the edge of the cliff and just as he is about to fall off, gently grab him by the back of his shirt and pull him back, softly stating, *Don't go that way, go this way.* Sometimes that boy listens to me and sometimes he certainly does not! If my mother ever thought I was stubborn then she should have met this guy. His streak is a mile long.

I never wanted him to be led down the garden path into the world of drugs and alcohol like so many before him. I did my best to deter him, to no avail. I told him he was better than all that. I told him that he was a shining star in the midst of some quickly fading ones. I told him that anyone can settle for being average but why would you if you possessed a natural talent to excel. I told him he was all of this and more. Still, he fell. I always knew I was no match for the stimulation that doing drugs offered a young and unsuspecting individual. He made a fool of himself and an even bigger fool of me. Sad but true.

His mother, the ultimate control freak, questioned my intentions toward him right from the start. That was her right as a mother. Can you only imagine her frustration? Here she was picking out a suitable step-father for her boys and had to hear my name over and over at the supper table. "You should've heard what Todd said today at work." After a while I suspect it must have burned her ass.

One of her remarks found their way to me. I didn't like the insinuation that my intentions toward her son were anything but honorable. Via email we chatted.

I rebutted with my popular reputation and regaled her with stories about the troubled youth I've worked with over the years and how any one of them would take a bullet for me. What a great man I am so why wouldn't she be grateful rather than suspicious of my motives. Here is her answer. *It is not a child's job to take a bullet for an adult; it is our responsibility to protect them at any cost, even our life.*

Wrong Lady!

Let's get one thing straight, I may take the time and effort to talk to these individuals and do so with the voice of reason but........I lay down my life for no one!

Wanna know why? Raise your own kid Lady! Where in the world did you ever get the idea that it is the responsibility of every adult in this world to look out for your kid? News flash: Most people are not that nice. Some want to have sex with your kid, take his money, pound his body or even taste his blood. Not everyone out there is your friend. Instead of you expecting me to pull your kid out of a well at great personal expense to myself, including possible death, do it yourself. Who will be there the next time he gets himself into trouble, who will save him if I died trying last time, some other unsuspecting asshole?

Like I said, "Raise your own kid Lady!"

Here is what I offer you and your kid. Some friendly advice. Teach him to make some good decisions. Instill in him that if something doesn't feel right, it probably isn't. Tell him that 'knowing when to leave is the smartest thing that a man can learn.' Allow him to make simple mistakes but teach him the consequences of his actions. That is exactly what I do for people. Rather than bake them a cake, I might teach them how to bake their own. In the process they feel good about themselves, see the fruits of their labour and end up with something sweet, so to speak.

I do love Spencer but more than that I respect him. I respect him enough to teach him to stand up for himself. If you should get knocked down, then get up again. Learn from your mistakes and from the mistakes of others. Try not to make the same mistake twice. Treat others in an honest and direct manner; they will ultimately respect you for it one day. Don't take foolish chances and do good things. Good advice right? You bet your ass it is!

I did do as she asked and backed off only to sadly see over the next year, that boy go down in a flood of alcohol and drugs which patrolled defiance and disrespect where his parents were concerned. Add in a few brushes with the law and you have a guy who barely resembles the kid who came thru the door years before. But guess who he calls when he was in dire straits? I have picked him up numerous times in the middle of the night, drunk out of his head. She's kicked him out on several occasions and shut off his phone. She relied on century old sayings. "If you live under my roof you will follow my rules." and "if you walk out that door do not even think about coming back."

Hey Spencer, my mother said the same things to me and as headstrong as I was, I didn't listen; I couldn't wait to get out from under her thumb. I swore the day I got married I would leave and not look back and I almost did it. After a while I was able to see finally that she was still in fact, my mother and she really did have my best interests in mind, it was just her approach was all wrong. Sound familiar?

The real irony of this situation is that someday Spencer's mother will be the ultimate interfering and controlling mother-in-law. The two sorry creatures that marry Spencer and his brother might not appreciate her......good intentions?

This was all before the accusation.

Richard Todd Canton

Spencer is off to college now and God I hope that boy uses some common sense. Boy, If you remember only one thing I have said over the years I hope it is this......"moderation is the key....and Spencer, if I never see you again in my life, please know that this man from where I am standing....loves you an awful lot..."

Perfect!

I am no expert on children as I have none of my own but I do come from a relatively large family and have an abundance of nephews and nieces. All of these people are quite interesting and each has their own story to tell. But, alas, one thing has always concerned me over the years and that is when people think their kids are better than others and more so when mothers think their children are perfect.

To my knowledge there only was one perfect person and that was Christ and look what they did to him.

That brings me to Spencer. In my last story I wrote story about him and how the pressures placed on him forced him to go against everything he was taught about family obligations and tradition. He was like a dog that had been chained up all summer and when the chain breaks, makes a run for it. He will return but not before running wild for a bit. That would be Spencer.

I met him when he came to work as a dishwasher in our restaurant at the age of sixteen. A nicer kid I have never met. He was clean, mannerly, considerate and enterprising. I was so impressed with him I took to the junior high where I worked for show and tell. I told the kids in grade six that if I could have a son then he is it! He was frugal with his money, active in sports, mostly hockey and he paid for his own vehicle. A far cry from the juvenile delinquents I was used to. Refreshing actually.

Spencer was not without faults the worst being a stubborn streak. When he made his mind up there was no changing it. No one knows this better than his mother. He fought her all the way. She of course blamed everyone else for his actions. This was the battle all through senior high. Add drugs and alcohol to the mix and pow, change came overnight. His priorities changed and reckless behaviour excelled. In fact it took over him. He did what he wanted to when he want to do it. The more his mother pushed, the more that boy resisted. Her hold on him went literally out the window. And him with it.

Then off to University........party time. By Christmas of that year the Dean had just about enough of Spencer and his antics, and he was eventually shown the door. Again in his mother's eyes it was his friends who ruined him. Hullo?

Now when it came to me I looked back on my own life. I did my best to get thru to him. I told him not to be a follower but to be a leader. Thinking now, I was just as stubborn and bull-headed at his age. I lived in the moment when my poor mother was looking at the big picture. I told her on many occasions to relax, the same words Spencer used on me.

Why I cared was beyond me. That boy has a father and a step father so why on earth would I or should I care? Well, he is the type that once he gets into your blood he is a little hard to resist. So every time he talked to me I found myself back on his side.

Spencer, now in his twenties is pulling it all together or doing his best to do so. I am glad but not without thinking about the title of this book and how it applies to him. Spencer you are not perfect but you are a wonderful and frustrating part of my life.

Love you Buddy!

One day and I know it is coming, Spencer will utter these words...."My son is so head strong and stubborn, he won't listen to word I say..."

Imagine that. I just hope I am around to hear them.

True Colors....

When John was born he inherited a pretty important name in our family. It seems that he has had to live up to that ever since. When he was as young as the age of five John showed us what type of resilient and tenacious individual he is. Juvenile Leukemia was his biggest enemy but he faced it, taking all that was thrown at him and then some, with nary a complaint.

Those of us who lament about our aches and pains were all brought to task when John showed us that even when he had reason to whine and complain, he didn't. He proved what a soldier he really was then and now.

John has proven that marching to the sound of your own drummer and being true to who you are is the way to go. That's why we are all so proud of him and why we love him so much.

His personality is colorful, while others may appear to be blue collar, redneck or just plain black and white in appearance, John's is like that of a rainbow. We all agree how beautiful rainbows are.

More than his personality or his good looks John is a beautiful individual because of his smile. It is contagious. His toothy grin forces each and every one of us to smile and that too is wonderful.

John is a kind and sensitive member of our family. He was unsure if everyone would still care as deeply as we do for him if his true colors were revealed. To us, his colors are beautiful.

John is proof that life doesn't have to be perfect to be wonderful.

John, you are wonderful.

John is a lesson teacher...he taught us not to complain about our lives when so many others out there are fighting for theirs.

Good morning Mrs Roberts

Come September when the big doors open it signifies that a new school year has begun. In the junior high where I worked it was always great to greet all who came through our doors. Grade nines were there for their final year in the junior high experience and the grade sixes were the newbies who had no idea what the next four years would entail.

Upstairs in the red neighborhood, called this because of the color of the lockers and floor tiles, is where the grade sixes congregate. There are a few nervous students and some confident ones as well. All are hoping this will be a great year and hopefully we will all make friends. Everyone finds their assigned seat in Mrs Robert's room.

This is quite the place mostly due to the atmosphere. It is a very inviting place and everyone is welcome. Mrs Roberts proves this on a daily basis when she says good morning. Not to the class but to every student individually. Good Morning Ariana, Good Morning Brenda, Good Morning Cody and so on until every student gets a Good Morning. She then turns to the EA in her classroom and says and Good Morning Mr Canton.

Good morning Mrs Roberts.

I am quite sure that she is aware of exactly how it makes everyone feel to be included in the classroom. Mrs Robert's has her fair share of experience. Every day began on a positive note. She would then ask if I had something to share with the class and it seems I did. I would talk about my family growing up, or my dog or my job as a part time waiter and how much I enjoyed that. The kids would sit like angels and listen to my every word. This was the beginning of my collecting stories that would eventually find their way to my very first book, Russell Street Memories.

Mrs Roberts encouragement on a daily basis was not only for the kids in the room but me as well and herself. A divorced mother of two young boys, she shared with the class what it was like to be on her own raising her sons and the struggles she faced. Never complaining she simply shared her life with us and taught us all that one must never give up. Let that be the most important of lessons learned.

Born into a French Acadian Catholic family in northern New Brunswick, Irma Legere was no stranger to the harsh winters and the struggles of surviving in this world. As a teacher it was her chance to share her life's lessons with not just the kids but with just about everyone she met.

Mrs Roberts sure loves her family. She is proud of the men her sons became and grandchildren are the real lights of her life. A focused and determined woman she rarely lets anything get her down. If it does she is not down for long. She believes that a belief in one's self and in God, you can get through anything, and she has.

I am proud to call Mrs Roberts my dear friend and to state that she has shown her support in so many ways. As a result, all I can do in return is to pay it forward.

Having said all this, I wish you well on your retirement and that because of you I will never forget to start my day off by acknowledging every person I meet with a sincere good morning.

My hands are tied

I got the call from my friend Jody, he was at the hospital, there had been an accident. His wife and eight year old son were in a collision on the highway just outside of Halifax. He was crying. Through his tears he begged me to come sit with him. I did. A shiver ran up my spine as I looked at Nathan lying there motionless.

His wife was in pretty bad shape but it was said she would survive. The boy on the other hand was not likely going to make it. They were told to call in the family. I was honored that he called me. Jody had always considered himself a loser and could not quite figure out why he was blessed with this child. His own father never treated him well and therefore it was his intention to never allow that man to use put downs that he used on his own son to ever fall on the ears of his own child. Therefore Nathan never knew his grandfather. I asked Jody if he wanted me to call him, he said it was entirely up to me. I did and sadly the grandfather chose not to come.

When you consider the type of person I am, the kind who always makes things all right, I felt my hands were tied where this was all concerned. All I could do for my friend was sit there and comfort him. I talked and I listened. I prayed. I am no stranger to prayer.

He told me how scared he was to become a father and how inadequate he felt he would be as a role model. He told me it was the words I had told him at the time that he carried with him in his soul ever since. God doesn't make mistakes and he sure didn't make one when he made you. Find your path, follow your dream. He did question why God would ever punish him by taking his son. I told him to think about it this way, that He blessed him when he gave him a son.

Children, I believe are on loan to you from God and when He is ready He takes them, it is His will. Jody watched the baby he was terrified to hold in his arms, blossom into the little boy who captured his heart for a lifetime. His smile, his mannerisms, he himself was just a reflection of his father and that was the real gift. Every time you consider yourself a loser just look into that little face that has eyes for only you and I swear something happens inside of you.

You will come to realize that this kid is the reason for you to get yourself out of bed every morning and for you to work overtime if need be, for you to take better care of yourself and for you to pull your selfish head out of your own ass and do what is needed to make sure that kid has everything he needs. He needs his Daddy.

Sadly, I stood beside my friend as we buried his boy. My breaking heart could do nothing to comfort him. All I could do was to continue to be his friend, their friend and to cherish the memory of the sweet angel that brought love into that man's heart. Jody spoke of how empty he felt inside and how he no longer wanted to go on. Who could blame him?

The first year after the boy died was the most difficult but then Jody told me how he handled it. He joined a group that talked to grieving parents and he was able to put to use his own experiences with losing the most precious thing in his life. He said he was honoring the little boy's memory by doing this.

The real lesson in life here is to take even the most devastating of situations in your life and make something good out of them. It's funny but they called me to help and it seems I may have gotten the most out of the whole situation.

Will the Real Todd Canton

Please Stand up!

I, Richard Todd Canton was born the fifth of seven natural children to Bert and Vivian Canton. Our family is continually expanding and each member of this end of the Canton Clan is interesting and unique. Some of us are outspoken and direct while others are shy and retiring. I am a perfect example of the middle child and a boy outnumbered by girls four to one. I believe myself to be honest, straight forward and direct. Some can handle that and others think I am too much for them. Well, might be true but all can agree that I am larger than life.

For as long as I can remember people have been trying to figure me out. Some can but most cannot. I believe that I am spontaneous and unpredictable to say the least. But don't take my word for it, here is what my friends think.

Todd Canton is a complicated individual and a private one. He shares only when he wants to and becomes quite evasive when he does not want to share. If you push him he will shut up like a clam. "True, I am a private person who does not want to be a burden to others. So I stand strong or at least I appear that way."

He grew up in a houseful of women and as a result is very sensitive and understanding. He inherited a natural intuition and uses it to the best of his ability. He seems to always have the correct thing to say and an intelligent way of saying it. Now catch him on an off day and that man will blow you away with his responses. His wit is quick and he is as sharp as a tack. "Overwhelmed might be a good word when describing my being under the influence of the female persuasion. But, in all honesty, I am really a Caspar Milquetoast, I bawl and cry at sentimental situations and tear up easily if there is evidence of real love in the room."

Todd Canton is a tall and handsome man. And a popular one. "Yup, I sure attract the ladies, and the gentlemen too." it has been both a blessing and a curse being a popular sort. It has certainly opened a few doors for me and closed a couple as well. However, I am pretty focused and determined so don't get in my way. I like to think that I can sit at any table and fit in. Learning when to talk and when to keep your mouth shut is a very valuable tool. I'll let you know if I ever master that."

"Everybody seems to think they know me and can predict what I am going to do or say next. Hell, I don't even know what's coming half the time so how could they?"

Todd Canton loves to cook and loves to eat. He is a great cook. When he sets his mind to it no one can beat him in the kitchen. When he steps up to the stove it is like a conductor ascending the podium. One never knows what concoction he will come up with. He makes a mean turkey stuffing, creamy whipped potatoes and of course, his own sultry gravy. He is great at desserts as well. Bread pudding with brown sugar sauce or cottage pudding is to die for. "He is a cake boss" says Jackie McKeown, his boss. He makes the moistest cakes. "That is quite a compliment considering that woman is married to a chef and she has traveled the world and eaten some fine cuisine. So if she says I am pretty good then I must be!"

"My family is a bunch of good cooks but it is from my wife that I learned to be a great one. That woman taught me to strive for excellence and led by example. She came honestly by it as her mother was a terrific cook as well."

Todd Canton has a marvelous sense of humor and is quick with the comments. "You call it humor, I call it funny sarcasm and a quirky way of looking at life. Not everyone however finds me hilarious but I am grateful for those who do. I will say one thing, had it not been for my unwavering ability to laugh at myself I could not have gotten this far in life. That and the fact that I am grateful for all the things I have but also for those I don't"

"I do not take necessary risks such as mountain climbing or car racing. I am too clumsy for all of that. I even have trouble on an icy driveway. I do have a great way with public speaking but have seriously had to learn when to shut my mouth. I have been arrested but I have never seen the inside of a jail cell. I have never had a pair of handcuffs on my wrists but I am told they hurt. I have also never had cancer nor a broken bone. I *have* had surgery on my left eye and many stitches as a kid. I have never used crutches nor a wheel chair but I sure am courteous to those who do. I have been on television in and out of the news and as a result I am aware of the public and all it has to offer. I have never been beaten or tortured but I was married for twenty-eight years. And as sick as I have ever been I have never been a guest inside the palliative care unit of any hospital."

So that brings me to the following statement *Stop complaining about your life when so many others are fighting for theirs!*

"I will say this, I have, on several occasions, walked through the fire and came out the other side. I have been judged and misjudged and I am stronger as a result. Therefore I am truly a grateful man."

Todd Canton has been told that he drives like Mr Magoo but that does not deter him. "Only once in my life have I gotten a ticket and that was in the last year, I would say that's pretty good."

Todd Canton loves the animal kingdom "If it is at all possible, in a former life I believe that I roamed the plains of Africa and was at one with the animals there. I am a firm believer that we can learn from the animal kingdom. I am a compassionate and gentle man but when it comes to any kind of animal torture or abuse I can very well become a murderous vigilante, so don't push it."

"I love my dog more than life itself. She needs me and I need her too! But, I would be remiss to think she will live forever. So I make the most of our days together. Alas I never wanted a dog. My wife did. I said No! So we got one. But, make no mistake, that is Daddy's baby"

Todd Canton is intelligent. "I like to think I am pretty smart and I have some great philosophies of life and some good advice. But do not ask for it if you cannot take the direct approach. A lot of people tend to ask your opinion but if you tell them something they don't want to hear..... well, you know the rest."

Todd Canton sure loved his mother "My Mom was an original. I can't stop talking about her. A strong and determined woman, nothing could keep her down. She had to face so much in her life. A widow, she also suffered the loss of business in a fire, financial ruin and yet she marched forward with a grand sense of who she was and showed us all the way. I admired her greatly. I wish she was here today so I could call her with my troubles. Her response would mostly be like 'don't call during Coronation Street'"

"She, our Mother, was the center of our lives. An amusing and intelligent woman, she had no fear. When left a widow in her forties with a whole houseful of kids to feed that woman marched forward with a 'grand sense' (there's that phrase again, very applicable) of who she was and with an intestinal fortitude that simply did not allow her to give up. I grew to admire her greatly. Dad died when I was eleven years old and it was around the age of fourteen that I began to notice just how strong she was. I commented that it was a wonder she didn't hop a freight considering all she had to face. Her reply was simply that her father was a coal miner who went underground and faced uncertainty and possible death but he had a family to feed, he didn't give up, why would I? And why would I?"

Todd Canton is a good friend. "I am a loyal friend and I expect the same in return. I can understand if you don't prefer to be my friend but if you are then I have certain expectations. First of all don't Lie! I am not a liar and I don't respect those who are. I have been lied to and lied about, despise them both. If you are my friend than I demand loyalty. If I am betrayed it not only makes me mad but it hurts. In return for loyal friendship I will be your confidant, defender, personal chef and loyal friend. Piss me off and see what happens."

Todd Canton is a good man. "I am a good man, my mother made sure of it." "And when I love someone they know it. I have never been afraid to show love and affection to those I hold dear."

Todd Canton is a music lover. "Even though I do not play any instruments I am quite musical. I also possess a great amount of musical knowledge where music is concerned so I might be the best 'phone-a-friend out there'. I am a fan of anything that is good and as much as I love today's music I am definitely a fan of the classics. As a few of you may know I have had a friendly obsession with singer Anne Murray for about forty years. I cannot imagine her music not being a part of my life. So therefore it is mostly the voice I love but I have been known to bust a move to just about any beat going."

Todd Canton can tell you the wildest stories and to this day no one is sure if they are true or not. "It has been proven on so many occasions that the truth is usually more bizarre than anything I could ever make up."

Todd Canton wears his wedding ring even though the two of them have separated. "Now this is a touchy subject. I will remove the ring when I and I alone am ready. You see, it was she who ended the marriage, I wasn't quite done. While I will admit that I was not the easiest person to live with, she stayed for twenty-eight years so that should tell you something. In our marriage she was all that mattered. She was also in charge. That woman knew when to rein me in and when to let me run."

"she is the only person outside of family that I ever truly loved and therefore it is not easy nor fair for me to pursue anyone else, at least not yet."

Todd Canton is unusual to say the least. "Ha ha, yup well now, quirky yes, unusual, hmm, I'll get back to you on that one!"

Todd loves his country. "Well, I am a proud Canadian but I do find that some of my fellow brothers and sisters are forgetting our national humility and resilience. The world we knew is falling apart and one of the reasons is that people no longer have hope for the future, or faith in God and when it comes to facing major issues lack the right problem solving skills.

I especially love the Maritimes. The people, the landscape, the water and I am definitely a fish lover so this is the perfect part of the country in which to reside. Lobster, yes please, scallops and halibut too! Clam chowder or deep fried clams, steamed mussels and mackerel.

Man I am getting hungry just speaking about it. Not to mention summer meals like freshly made potato salad and hodge-podge or winter meals like beef stew or corned beef and cabbage. Todd Canton loves to eat. "I sure have a big appetite where food is concerned. If I read a magazine and I see the pictures of food, my mouth waters. I go to sleep at night, dream about food and I wake up hungry.

Ok, you got me started now with breakfast, fluffy scrambled eggs or over easy or even boiled, I love eggs! (don't forget Eggs Benedict or poached eggs on toast). Pan fried potatoes, lightly toasted bread and orange juice. Then there is lunch, chicken salad sandwiches, homemade soup, just about any kind. I love pork chops smothered in sauteed onions and mushrooms served with boiled new potatoes and any kind of veggies. And then there is roast beef, and chicken and lasagna and goolash and roast turkey....ok, ok I'll stop!"

Todd Canton is not afraid to speak up if he sees an injustice. "I am a firm believer that God did not make me this large and give me a big mouth if he expected me not to use either. For instance, I cannot stand bullies, not in life, work or in school so I confront them. I absolutely cannot tolerate anything being done to animals, children old people or any other being that is on the receiving end of anything bad. I will speak up, and do so in a reasonable way. I am a firm believer that there is a right and a wrong way to say anything."

So, do you have me figured out? Not likely but I will say this, I am strong in my opinions and convictions. I truly believe that we as human beings should do what's right, no matter the cost.

Alcohol:

Because no Story Ever Began with a Salad!

I like beer. I am not a wine drinker nor am I a connoisseur of whiskey or rum. Not only do I not like the taste, frankly, I cannot handle them. So like I said, I like beer. I tend to get full easy and then off to bed I go. I really should eat first so that I don't end up with a hangover. Smart eh? Not always. Once I drank too much and slipped on some wet leaves and while not breaking it, put my finger out of joint. Ouch! I have also been inebriated enough to scrape my shins, lose my footing and fall and even bumped my head. But, I have also been smart enough to know my limits and get myself home and into bed.

I have given new meaning to the name "dancing fool" buy applying alcohol to the music. Sometimes I pull it off on the dance floor and sometimes I get pulled off the dance floor. Moderation being the key to success.

I make it a point to never drink and drive but if you ever saw me drive some days, it might have been wiser for me to have a couple and maybe then I might be a little more relaxed behind the wheel. However, I am pretty good at letting the cabbie do the driving while I am drinking.

Living in the Maritime provinces it seems like music and humour and alcohol go hand in hand. Beer fits nicely in your hand, music in your ears and heart and humour because it can truly get you through anything. If it doesn't the alcohol will or at least blurr it enough so you don't care for a while.

Here's a question. Is it me or the alcohol? Alcohol causes many things. It makes good times better, tense times calmer and bad times worse. If you are truly facing a troubled time, it might be wise to keep your head clear until the worst is over. Then it would be the right time to raise your glass and to celebrate.

I have seen marriages break up over alcohol. I have seen people get together because of it as well. I have seen it lower inhibitions, enlarge tempers, affect moods both good and bad and maybe just maybe, relax the tense.

I have made some bad decisions while under the influence. I have raided gardens as a teen, picked *off limit* flowers as an adult, said things I wish I hadn't and done things I wish I never have but I have never contemplated murder, used a firearm, put anyone in danger physically or sexually while under the influence but I have been accused of it. I have however, allowed others to entice me into some delicate situations for which I shake my head later. I have been known to snore decibels while passed out and gotten up long enough to barf and then fall back to a comatose state. I have woken up to dry drool on my mouth and pillow and I have felt bad enough that I swear I never will do it again. Still do though.

I have also been the only sober person in the room. Now there is an education of sorts and the main question you might ask is "Do I look that stupid when I drink?" chances are yes and maybe even more so.

What I am trying to say is, I am the same man I have always been whether or not I have a beer, well maybe a little more of an asshole.... sorry for that.

Hmm I sure could use a cold one.

A Piece of Paper

When my wife was passed over for a promotion because she required a degree, I thought to myself, Wow it's just a piece of paper compared to the years of experience that girl has in the computer business. She has proven herself on several occasions that she is well versed and knowledgeable in everything that she does. However, that piece of paper was the only thing that was standing between her and the promotion, so she got one. Upon achieving it, also gained confidence enough to look for a job elsewhere.

It also got me thinking that paper plays a more of a major role in our lives without our really taking the time to really ponder it. A piece of paper from your mother excused you from class and one from your doctor got you excused from work. In fact, those pieces of paper held so much power that no one could dispute it.

A winning lottery ticket is a piece of paper. It is one that could change your whole life in either a good or a bad way. A divorce paper could as well.

A pay-cheque is a much anticipated piece of paper, so is a driver's licence, a vehicle permit, and finally a death certificate. OK that one is not as anticipated as the rest.

A pink slip is another piece paper no one wants, but a fifty dollar bill in this country is a pink piece of paper that everybody wants.

Paper grows on trees and trees give us oxygen. That makes us all breathe a little easier, so to speak.

All of us want to be paper thin, at least at some time in our lives and then there's the way we paper our walls, get our news from the newspaper. We need paper to blow our noses on when we have a cold, we line the bird cage with paper and then there's the always useful toilet paper.

Ransom notes are on paper, so are love letters, gifts are wrapped in tissue paper, fresh meat in brown paper, and then the best communication tool in school, the paper airplane.

That brings us to the union of marriage and all it offers. A piece of paper changes you from a single man to a husband, or from a husband to an involuntary single man.

So I guess I gave you something to think about. So the next time someone favours living together over the commitment of marriage by stating that it's the same thing and that the marriage certificate is "just a piece of paper", what they might really mean is something that my Aunt Francess said on several occasions, "why buy the cow when you are getting the milk for free."lol

and always remember, my stories might not be worth the paper they are written on......or are they?

I Love you more than I can say....

When it comes to love, I am no stranger. I was lucky, I grew up in a house full of love. Our mother was the ultimate in protecting and nurturing giving to each of us what she thought we needed at the time. In return she was the one who was needed. Like a mother hen she kept her clutch close to her breast and for those of us who felt it important to break away, let us go. Some stayed but me, well I couldn't wait to go.

I was as independent and determined as she was so we often clashed. She did however, always made me feel respected despite any difference in opinion and there was plenty of that. That is what happens when two strong minded individuals live under the same roof.

So out into the big world I went leaving all the shy members of my family behind, looking for my destiny, and following my path, my way. I have been quite fortunate in my travels. I got to meet a lot of interesting individuals and see some wonderful sights. But, and there is always a but, no matter where I traveled and no matter what I have seen, my thoughts run home to you Mother.

In my mind and in my heart I run home to our house on Russell Street and to the smell of Red Rose tea steeping on the stove. To the warm breezes that swept across the marsh and kept us all breathing good clean air. From the dog-berry trees to the blueberry fields and back, it means nothing without you there.......

Mother, I love you more than I can say.

A Winter In Amherst

after the winter we all have braved I am sure the reader lets out a groan at the very thought of snow.

Winter, ah, what fun when you're a kid. There's skating, sliding, coasting down the hills on your toboggan, and of course, hockey. Winter is not so much fun when you are older, mostly due to the fact that we, the people of today, are busier, we have less time to do the things we want to, and have so much more to worry about. We also don't want to bundle up like our mothers used to make us when we were going out the door. We now rely on the warmth of our vehicles and a ticking clock to get us where we are going.

Lately I dread winter because it slows me down. I hate driving on the highway because all I ever seem to hear is about accidents and tragedies that result because of slippery roads. So we, tend to take it easier during those winter months. Now with global warming and all that, we may or may not have any snow at all. When it does come however, it comes!

One winter in Amherst especially comes to mind. The winds that blow across the Tantramar Marshes bring with them a lot of snow and freezing winds, you know, real winter. We had suffered through a few days of snowfall, leaving Amherst in a real standstill. It took the plows days to get everyone dug out. When that was done the snow banks on the side of the road were so huge that you had to be warned by your mother **not to touch the telephone wires**, while walking to school. It's almost unbelievable today unless you think about White Juan. Kids today don't know what winter is.

In West Amherst there lies the Chignecto Bird Sanctuary, or as we called it, the GLEN. The Glen in it's own right is a very beautiful haven for water fowl. Lakes upon tree lined lakes of beautiful clean water and as I said, hundreds of species of birds flock there, making their homes, feeding on the water life in the lakes, and live a peaceful life under the watchful eye of man. In winter the lakes freeze and if it stayed something like twenty below for ten days, then it was safe to skate on. For me it was a little scary at first, because I could feel the ice cracking under my feet and of course, there were always horror stories about people falling through the ice. Who knows if they were true or not?

Anyway, tobogganing was my favorite thing to do, and the hills at the sanctuary were steep so with all that snow and such big hills, down we would go. Flying through the air at uncontrollable speeds made your heart race, your adrenalin kept you warm and the struggle of re-climbing the hills made you tired. Loads of fun. My friend Brian and I or my cousin Edward would quite often walk across the marsh, pulling behind us, our toboggans. My sister Ruth would quite often want to tag along but I didn't want her to because then I was responsible for her, and I'll tell you now, Mother held us responsible for each other. However, one day, we let her tag along.

As we approached the hill I told her she was too little to slide down the hill on the back of our toboggan. She didn't like that. *Too bad,* I thought, because, only two on the toboggans at a time, three would not be safe. Well guess what, we did it. First Edward, then me, and then Ruth. As the three of us soared toward the unknown, down the cold and snowy hills at great speed we hit a bump with resounding consequences. I fell off and rolled down the hill, Edward went the distance, but Ruth literally flew through the air, landing face down in the snow with a thud, unconscious. I was sure she was dead.

As I made my way down the slippery hill I approached her lifeless body, calling her name. Half crying, I knew this was all my fault and that's when Ruth pulled her snow covered and bloodied face up and shouted "Let's do it again!" I looked at Edward in disbelief and he at me.

We did it again.

As the Crow Flies

My backyard is a veritable playground for birds and small wildlife. One never knows what they will see when you look out my kitchen window. Wild partridges are abundant at this time of year. The neighborhood cat usually frightens them off. Then there's the sparrows, the starlings, beautiful blue jays, wild canaries, you name it. Most of them take advantage of our trickling pond and all it has to offer. It must be fascinating as our cat never leaves the window, she enjoys the show.

Once in a while a deer or two will wander through our property looking for fallen apples. But it is a squirrel that has made it's home in the neighbor's barn that fascinates me the most. What a busy little guy he is scampering about our yard, gathering scraps of food that he can store to get him through the long winter. That's one thing man and animal have in common, we are all trying to weather the weather.

Last Sunday during a routine clean up in the kitchen there was a bag of unused home-made bit & bites that would not likely be of any use to anyone. So, I thought the birds might like it and they tend to make the best of anything at this time of year. It cannot be easy for them..

So, I use my best arm to hurl handfuls of this rather tasty snack as far up the hill as I can. If it's too close to the house it may go unnoticed so I did my best to get it into the clearing. Not a bird in sight. Well, I thought to my self, it'll take a little time but someone will discover it. Well, not too long afterward, the little squirrel came gliding down the hills of white and JACKPOT! Pine nuts and peanuts and hickory sticks and pretzels and cheezies, what more could a hungry soul ask for? The first thing he did was taste a cheezie, it must've tasted good because he grabbed the next one in his cheeks and up the hill he went straight to his home in the barn. Back and forth the little prince scampered filling his cheeks and returning to his nest.

Before long a bird or two noticed the orange dots in the snow and swooped down for a treat. First a mourning dove who cooed at the very sight of the feast and then let it known to her friends what was upon them. Then a blue jay, these birds are famous for chasing all others away but this guy wasn't true to form. He kept a respectful distance from the others. All is well. Then, as fate would have it, the neighbor's cat spotted the clutch of fowl and did his best to make his way down the snowy hill through the crunchy stuff, of course, giving himself away. Off they flew, no massacre here thank goodness. I guess cats don't care for bits & bites so he didn't stick around for long. The feast resumed.

But as the crow flies it is usually a warning to all. Danger is near. These birds are big as chickens, the menace of the sky, terrorize the neighborhood, tear open garbage bags, threaten the existence of all those who live around them. No wonder Alfred Hitchcock chose the likes of them to terrorize movie audiences. I think they would love to have feasted on a little squirrel gumbo and probably would have had they not noticed the strewn about treats. So as fate would have it, the rest of this food was cleaned up by these massive scavengers leaving nothing but a hint of orange dust on the crusty snow. But I will tell you one thing, there's one fat and happy little squirrel in a cozy barn up the hill.

Just Between Friends...

When my friend Scott and his girlfriend broke up, I was devastated. Okay, really it is none of my business but I love them both and I am smart enough to know that apart there is no telling which direction their lives will take. She was the first to start dating and it hit him very hard. "What did you think?" she asked "That I would be Todd Canton pining away in my apartment!"

Ouch! Sad but true.

It has been three years since the two of us have separated and yet I find it difficult to move on. I guess deep inside I thought I never thought the two of us would ever part. I was silly in the fact that I thought she and I would last forever. Silly man, silly dreams!

I know the days of staying together forever no longer seem in fashion but I have always considered myself to be out of the norm on just about every level. Few would argue I am sure. Also the fact that she and I had an intensely private life put us under scrutiny. Since no one really knew what went on behind closed doors, they could only assume.

So Scott says to me, Do you think she ever loved me? Yes but she loves herself too. She had no choice but to save herself in the end.

She was patient and understanding but every time you allowed your moods to take over and in doing so was disregarding her feelings.

Well why didn't you tell me all of this? I never saw any of it for sure until it was too late.

She is a living breathing human being with feelings, needs and concerns. If you choose to overlook those things then she will have no choice but to find another way to have her needs met.

What I did not know was that all the things I said just between friends I could apply to my very situation. Imagine that.

Perhaps I should have followed my own advice.

COAL

When a young Vivian Gillis left the town of Springhill, Nova Scotia in 1948 to be married, she so looked forward to her life, yet longed for home. The close knit ties of a coal mining family are carefully interwoven and uneasy to sever, perhaps due to a lot of pain and anguish. The kind of pain and anguish that goes along with the tragedies afforded coal mining families.

The depth and darkness of the Cumberland mine has been described over and over as the blackest of black, the loneliest of lonely and the coldest of cold. But it is with those above ground that the worry sets in and the waiting takes place. Everyday the miners dig a little deeper, miles beneath the earth's crust.

Vivian Gillis's father Dan and his brothers were all the men of the deep mines. All bore the scars of this difficult and weary life. Most of them aged before their time, suffered illness later in life but coal mining was in their blood. A hard old life for these resilient and valiant men. As Vivian Gillis and her husband Bert were in the process of creating a family Amherst, tragedy struck. Fully pregnant with her fourth child the news came from Springhill. November 1956, a devastating mine explosion. Vivian Gillis, beside herself with grief, waited for her husband to come home and safely deliver her to her family.

The Cumberland County drive from Amherst to Springhill is a beautiful one at the best of times but in the Fall is it is just short of spectacular. The color of the leaves, the ones that hadn't fallen, were able to channel her thoughts back to her childhood and the many strolls she would take through the untouched forest. The sound of the sirens broke her concentration and brought her back to reality. As they got closer and closer to the town the traffic thickened. Cars, trucks, police, fire engines, ambulances. Dense smoke hung in the air and the stench of death was all about. This dreary vision of Springhill is one that Vivian Gillis would hold in her soul forever. The fact that her father was in the mine and was lucky enough to escape with his life was comforting but there were so many more.

Tragedy brings people out in the streets. All met near the face of the mine. Doctors, miners, draegermen, business men and the intense and profound sound of crying. Just as they were able to bring some to the surface word came that friends and family alike had lost someone dear.

A cousin, an uncle, a friend, gone. Such is the life of a miner's family. Blood and bone is the price for coal, pain and suffering linger in your soul. Vivian Gillis, like every other true Springhiller took the disaster in stride. She supported those who needed it, fed the families of the miners, opened her family home to those who needed a hot thermos of tea or a place to lie down. The media swarmed the town, support came from all over the world, and as families came together to say goodbye to the lost ones, Vivian Gillis went home to Amherst to have her baby. Naturally upset by all that went on, Vivian suffered complications that sent her to the doctor. Blood pressure at an alarming rate might very well cause the death of her baby or even take her own life. So, she had to settle herself down. She did, and a few weeks later she held a baby girl in her arms.

As life moved forward Vivian and Bert and their four children lived a moderately quiet life. It was probably not their intention to have any more children but a couple of years later there she was, full with child, 1958, when the underground bump shook the town of Springhill nearly upside down. This time 74 men were killed, the other 100 survived, some barely. Loved ones collected their beaten and broken and the whole town mourned the losses together. This time the results were devastating enough to make the decision to permanently close the mines.

When one thinks about the disasters that we as a world community, have had to face, it might be true that it produces some of the strongest and most resilient people. I don't think anything compares to the souls of the families of coal miners. Work, blood, sweat, worry, tears, death and more tears. Despite the obvious dangers involved, their abounds among them a true sense of the value of life, laughter and love. Those brave hard working men like her father Dan Gillis, his brothers Angus and Hughie, and sisters Francess Gillis, and Mary Soppa were determined to secure a better life for their children, far from the darkness of the mines. Dan Gillis didn't want Vivian to be a miner's wife. To him, there had to be a better life outside the walls of Springhill and there was. I should know, I was that baby.....

Vivian Gillis is my mother.

This Story Has No Happy Ending

I warn you now this story has no happy ending. When my very black cat India died after living with me for fourteen years, I cannot lie, was heartbroken. The following year was torture for me because she wasn't just a pet, she was my little girl. Loss of a loved one of any kind is painful and the best advice I can offer is to look forward and to get on with your life. Great advice, huh?

In an effort to end my grief my wife shocked me by bringing home a kitten for my birthday. I honestly could have killed her, my wife I mean, not the kitten. I not only did not want another pet, I absolutely didn't want anything to remind me of exactly what I had lost. I truly wanted to be alone in my grief. Grieving is nothing new to me. I lost my father at an early age, my grandparents, friends, my mother and now my little girl. I knew that time would take care of me and besides, I have a dog. But, my wife, God bless her, thought this wild and crazy (which she calls feisty) tortoise shell cat would fill the void.

At first I couldn't stand the sight of her. There she was all different colors blended into a dark coat and a yellow patch over one eye. I couldn't even see her face clearly. Sherry called her Chloe and I called her Butterscotch Face. She was constantly disrupting the older cats, running and jumping about and crashing into things. Not the brightest little thing, I thought to myself. She was always running from food dish to food dish diving in and helping herself to the other cats dinners. Much to their dismay I might add. And she was clumsy too! Continually knocking things over and smashing most that she touched, all I could think of was why would someone do this to me? I know my wife meant well but, hullo? It is quite possible that not one thing in our house has not had a paw print on it.

As the year progressed, Chloe, the wildcat grew to be larger than all the other house-cats and despite her juvenile approach to life she was fast becoming one of the pack. I thought for sure they all hated her but..... I don't know yet why the long established cat family in our home would allow her to join the group but they did. Robbie, my reclusive cat warmed up to her the most. This was something I never expected but then again I am constantly amazed by the animal kingdom, whether they be domestic or wild. Maybe as the oldest of our cats he was amused by the tireless, and I mean tireless energy of this youngster.

Then one day it happened, she went too far, she knocked the Christmas tree down. I was furious, my wife was upset but still she found it entertaining. Entertaining? You've got to be kidding, I was adamant that this crazy feline was to go. I want to tell you that I have never turned away an animal and for me to even say this was really shocking to all involved. But my wife stood strong and I of course backed down. I guess I could learn to live with her, I am sure the crazy nut would outgrow the behavior and even the vet promised after Chloe was spayed that on or around 18 months she would calm down. Ha!

Anyway, as these stories go, I had a change of heart brought on by a choking noise in the middle of the night. I sprang from my bed toward a gasping and crying kitten that had gotten herself into something she shouldn't have. After a few quick moves on my part, I held in my arms what I had forgotten. This was a baby and I was her daddy. My heart was melting and I was able to look at her differently. I instantly learned to love that multi colored face. Will she ever take the place of my India? Nope! Chloe has made a place of her own.

Oh Yeah, I lied about the happy ending, sorry!

How much is that doggie in the window?

In an effort to make my dog's life as comfortable as possible I spoke to my wife about putting in a window seat so that the little dog, a sh'tzu, could have something to keep her occupied while we were at work.. She loved looking out the window from the end of the chesterfield, surveying her neighborhood. She would do this for hours quite often falling asleep.

Building a window seat is no problem for my wife as she is very handy around the house. More so than I am. But it would also mean a disturbance to our living quarters. My wife and I and our dog are not the only ones who live in our house. We share our home with five indoor house-cats. Their ages range from twelve months to twelve years. Each comes with their own funny quirks and some even come with some not so funny quirks. That folks, is another story. Still, my wife and I came up with a suitable solution by re-building a coffee table with a secure position beneath the window, complete with a soft pillow some five times the dog's size. What a life!

My dog Rozie is very special to the two of us. She is our first and probably our only dog. She has a great playful personality and loves to show it off. She knows her place in our home and she keeps my wife and I in line. It was my wife who insisted on getting a dog, I never wanted one. Too much work I thought to myself and besides, we both work. Still, we got one. My diligent wife crate trained the dog at first and made sure all her needs were taken care of, no matter what time of day or night. I couldn't help myself, I thought she was pretty cute. What I didn't know was that the dog had eyes for me. Although Mother was the one who took care of her, it was my arrival each day that the young dog anticipated. Anticipated with such warmth and love, I couldn't help but return the feelings. Soon, I was hooked. This was now, and will always be, my baby girl.

There's a price to pay for love. Every morning at six my little alarm clock wakes me up. "Come on Daddy! It's time to run up the road." While Daddy doesn't always feel like it, I had to realize that these things just have to be done. To tell the truth, if you knew what a selfish person I am, no one would ever think I would take the time 365 mornings a year to take care of business with that little dog. But, I have a responsibility to face. So, onward and upward we go. We've braved the cold, the snow, winds and rain and that was just yesterday. On the freezing days Rozie doesn't want to step outside let alone the trek up the road, so we tried to do our business in the back yard. It doesn't work! So, like a big monster I force her to face the elements, telling myself that she is an animal after all, and that the two of us can make it. Then come the dramatics. If her paw is cold or frozen she lifts it in an effort to shield it from the weather and then she whimpers softly which pulls on my heart strings. "Okay then" I think to myself. "Today you can poop in the house."

"Okay, wait a minute, no that's not okay. She's a dog and I am a man. I am the one who should be whimpering. She's a dog, for heaven's sake, they poop out side, that's what dogs do!" "Let's get this over with and I'll take you back home and you can lie in the warmth of a sunbeam shining in our living room window, and relax on a window seat that Mother fashioned, and watch the whole world go by, while the two of us are out working so that we can provide you with such a lavish life. Cool?

Also, for what it's worth, other dogs don't live like this" I might as well be talking to the wall.

I honestly wonder if she's worth all this. And then something happens. After an exhausting day of neighborhood watching, rounding up cats, greeting guests, sleeping in a sunbeam, eating a healthy supper and taking an evening walk, she cuddles up to her Daddy with sleepy eyes. Uh, oh, there's that face and that love I was talking about. My little girl, my baby dog. She needs me, she loves me, and just when I needed to be appreciated. So I had better get some rest. After all, tomorrow is another day.

So I ask, "How much is that Doggie in the window? Why, she's worth everything to me.

Love Daddy!

Double Wedding

When a young Vivian Gillis moved from the small coal mining town of Springhill to the more cosmopolitan and busier town of Amherst to work, it was like any impressionable young woman going to a strange city, filled with adventure and hope for the future.

She was all grown up and her family couldn't have been prouder of her. Vivian Gillis, at her family's urging was determined to not become being a miner's wife. She was an educated young woman who was fortunate enough to have the chance to venture out into the big world. Amherst and Springhill are only 16 miles apart but Amherst was a lot larger and there were certainly a lot more people and business opportunities there. She found a place to live and board and formed a lasting friendship with the family. The Goldsmiths were practising Catholics like herself, and held family in high regard. The two daughters Marjorie and Patricia became like sisters to Vivian. This made life bearable as she so badly missed the family she left behind in the close knit coal mining community.

Vivian joined the workforce as a sales clerk in the hardware business. Douglass Hardware on Victoria Street in Amherst was a well respected and thriving business. She did her best to fit in. Vivian had quite an outgoing personality and it paved the way for her in a business world that was predominantly ruled by men. Still she found her place.

How to treat people was an asset but knowledge a better tool. She worked hard to learn as much about the hardware business as she could. Her efforts paid off one day in particular. As a customer approached the desk, she immediately asked him if she could serve him. He was quick to say he much preferred a male clerk. "Of course" she said and motioned for one of the boys to wait on the customer. Not one to show any kind of emotion to the public, she allowed the sexist remark to pass and buried her head in her work. After a question or two from the customer the young clerk approached Vivian for the answer. She complied. Again the young man had a dilemma and she then too was helpful. It was after a third request that the young man was quick to inform the customer and the entire listening audience, ***"she knows more than me!"***

There's a lesson in there somewhere.

A young man who was working in the warehouse of Douglass Hardware took a liking to the bright young woman. He found her interesting. Her quick wit and outgoing personality was something that drew him closer to her. He, Bert Canton, was a shy individual who was mesmerized by this striking young woman. The two fell in love. By this time Patricia Goldsmith had met the man of her dreams, a Frenchman Rene Richard. Marjorie began dating Jack Lane and so there was no doubt about it, love was in the air. Talk of marriage between the three young women was a daily topic over coffee, who would be asked first?

Vivian Gillis and Bert Canton were well matched and in everyone's eyes, and it became evident that the two of them would eventually wed. Vivian herself knew this was the only man she would ever love. He wasn't like any of the others she had been associated with. There was definitely something in his expression that spoke directly to her. Despite their vast differences the two of them knew each other was the one.

Pat and Rene were anxious to get on with their lives. He so wanted to take her to his homeland in Quebec and she was willing to follow him wherever he went. So marriage plans were in the works. Despite the fact that the two came from totally different cultures, love conquered all. Rene gathered what family he had nearby and Pat did the same but it was when it was suggested that a double wedding take place that things really began to get moving. While not everyone might agree on more than one bride in the room, it turned out to be a great opportunity to get the two shyest men to the altar, while allowing two bright and intelligent women to do the same. Never was there an ounce of competition between the two, it really would be pointless.

As the November weddings drew near, Mrs Goldsmith sat Vivian down for a talk. "I just wanted you to know that since you don't have a mother of your own to see you proper, I will sit with pride and keep an eye on you like a mother would, because I would be proud to have you as a daughter." Such kind words on the woman's part only deepened the affection Vivian held for the whole family. Mrs Goldsmith opened her doors to the Gillis family and although Aunt Francess would never have admitted it, she too appreciated the gesture. She was after all, the one who raised Vivian when her mother saw it fit to exit the baby's life, leaving her in the hands of the Gillis family.

Their girl was getting married and this was a reason to rejoice. Everyone was so very proud of Vivian and the choices she made in life. She met a man they all approved of and that was not an easy feat in a family that never agreed. Still, there they all were, bursting with pride at such an event.

In the wee hours of a November morning, the Cantons, the Goldsmiths, the Richards, and the Gillis families all gathered at Saint Charles Catholic Church in downtown Amherst Nova Scotia, where Miss Patricia Goldsmith became Mrs. Rene Richard and Miss Vivian Gillis became Mrs. Bert Canton and the rest, Ladies and Gentlemen, is history, mine.!

I was told as a child that all of us kids were brought into the world by love and love alone and have been fortunate to have lived a life filled with a real sense of life, laughter and love.

I am a Survivor!

I think one of the most important things you will do in your lifetime is survive, and to keep marching forward. When a loved one passes away it is written that he or she is survived by.....well let's be honest, the dearly departed, their troubles are over. It is us that are left behind to carry on and it is not as easy as it looks and it is not as easy as people make it sound.

Accept it and move on, you are told on a few occasions, those words seem harsh at the time but prove that over time we become accepting of the hand we are dealt. My advice to anyone who has been hit by tragedy, please stay strong, and muster the strength to stand tall. I had to and even when I thought I could go on no longer a kind word or gesture from friends and family made me want to continue.

Now suffering what I went through pales in comparison with what a lot of other people have had to endure. We, in this part of the world seem to make things all about us and in many situations, rightfully so. But, don't feel too sorry for yourself because your friends will start running for the hills. They will be there when you are down but try not to burden them with too much of what is going on because you will end up forcing their hand and in doing so you hear those words.... accept it and move on.......am I right or what?

Now that we have made that point, here is the real lesson in being a survivor. Teach. Educate the portion of the population that you are indeed a survivor and that you will continue to be one. Share the wisdom of your experience and allow others to see that they too can endure all that is thrown at them. Allow them to know that even when they think they are at their wits end, they are stronger than they even know. I speak of what I know.

And really on the major scale of things, what of real importance will really matter in a hundred years? I want to remember any mountains that I had to climb to be just a part of a journey that took me to many interesting and challenging corners of this complicated world.

Life really is worth living and it doesn't have to be perfect to be wonderful.

Just Plain Betty

Every once in a while I take inventory of my life and most times I walk away grateful. My mother taught me at an early age to be grateful for what you have, not what you do not have. Great advice.

This is what I have today. A healthy and decent approach to life. Despite any rough roads I have traveled, life really is still worth living. I have a positive attitude and look forward to every day. I love my dog Rozie who runs my life. I also have the privilege of calling myself father to the most dramatic cat actress, Bette Davis. Most people pronounce it "Bett" but really it's just plain Betty.

Plain might be the word to describe her. She tan in colour, with light green eyes. Oh those eyes, they were blinking at me this morning from the comfort of our day bed in the sun room. This very yellow room absorbs the morning sun in such a way that it makes it probably the most peaceful and comfortable room in our house. At least my sleeping lamb, Bette thinks it does.

This is where Bette has chosen to spend most of her day. Since she is an indoor cat she has mastered the art of relaxing. I am sure that over the years I have learned the true meaning of comfort from that cat. Sunbeams are an asset to a perfect afternoon nap. Fresh water please, in the bowl would be nice but if I have to, I will drink it from the dripping faucet. Also, feed me please when my belly is hungry, I'll let you know when. Along with all of this, I want to reserve the privilege of walking on you at any time, snuggling into your neck early in the mornings, follow you around if I so desire and ignore you completely if that suits me. Are you cool with all this Daddy?

Yes dear, I am.

I know you love me, she says with those eyes, the famous Bette Davis eyes. Those same eyes that reeled in the movies goers for decades now call the attention of the only man in this girl's life, Daddy. Now you know, in the cat kingdom, there is no relationship between a male and the kittens. Mother does all the work. But in this case, because it suits her, Daddy is the one who carries her when she needs to be carried, protects her from the others when she has been bullied and loves her, just because.

Bette Davis does not meow. She doesn't have to. If she makes any kind of sound I come running. I guess a better way to put it is 'if she speaks, I listen'. Once, I heard a mournful cry from behind the couch. It seems she had her claw caught in the fabric and couldn't get free. She made her presence known and Daddy came to the rescue. In doing so I wanted to hug her and soothe her, she simply would have none of that. Bye, off she scampered to another room.

Some might say so but I assure you that Bette Davis is not a vain cat. She is simply the Queen of our household. She dominates the upstairs and is not afraid to put the run to the other cats that live in our house, is she so desires. Bette has had her portrait done by Robb Scott but she doesn't care about a picture. Why would you stare at that when you have the real thing in the room. I suppose.

So, it was November of '97 when I brought her home under my shirt. I remember rushing by my wife hoping she wouldn't take notice of the squirming rascal I brought home to join the brood. Instead Bette popped her head out at the perfect moment only to make Mommy melt. It was inevitable that she and I be together from the moment our eyes met. Okay, she was a little resistant but I managed to win her over. Over the years she has found comfort in my arms, on my chest, around my neck and in my heart. Will she live forever? No. Will I cry when she goes, you bet!

I cry now if I think about it too much.

However, there is always today and that brings me to that word again, grateful. I have the day off work and have it to myself. It's hot today so any lounging today will probably be done in the living room where the air conditioner is. And after lunch maybe a nap on the bed. Daddy, Rozie the dog and my lovely, my beautiful, just plain Betty!

Life is good.

Ladies and Gentlemen, the most dramatic cat actress in the world, Miss Bette Davis: 1997-2015

2015 makes year number 18 for the little girl I brought home under my shirt. I am proud of her resilience and tenacity and sheer stubbornness. But, like all things, she took a turn for the worse and in her mother's arms, said goodbye. But man, what a life. She was the one over the years that cost us the least yet taught us the most. I have no doubt in my mind that Rory was waiting at Rainbow Bridge and when he saw her no doubt fell on his side and offered her a friendly paw the way he did when he met her the very first time I brought her home.

Just A Pet

It was my wife who brought the black and white cat home. She had seen her run over on Prince Street and left for dead. It upset her terribly that people just drove around the obviously injured animal. "NO COMPASSION IN THIS TOWN" she shouted out in a letter to the paper. That caused a whole series of events that led to us taking this 'broken doll' home with us.

Paige is someone I felt never quite belonged to us. She was not one of our babies, she was a pet. For the next nine years she resided with us. She was not affectionate, well not really. She was very vocal. She made it known to us when she was hungry. Soft cat food please in the evenings, hard stuff throughout the day. Then I will enter a world of slumber and comfort in the basement of our house and as long as you two will have me, I will stay. But, and there's always a but, I am just a pet. I am not your personal property.

Paige is the one that stands out the most in our house. She photographs the best so it was always her photo that we showed off. The others girls like India and Bette may have been my personal babies but their photographs left a little to be desired. Her spirit shone through.

Paige was also never one to back down from a fight or to make her presence known unless it were to her liking. I am sure you all know what I mean. However, the nine years she spent with us were interesting just like she was and I grew to admire her. She was a great pet.

Where she ever came from was a mystery to us. Not something one likes to think about because what if the unthinkable happens, that someone discovers that we have her and they come to get her? Oh no, I thought to myself, we are definitely attached to her and her to us. Lay low, after all her life here is better than what we had imagined she came from.

Fate is fickle. Once, in a daring escape she wandered around for day or two. We placed Lost Cat posters and got many calls. To our surprise she found her way home to her original owners. They wondered where she had gone all those years ago and we wondered where she came from. Because of their kindness, Paige was able to come back home to us. They knew we had taken good care of her and why break up a happy home. Kind, right?

Paige was a genuine beauty. I tried on several occasions to tell her so and to show her how much I enjoyed having her join our family and to convey to her that I wanted her to live out the rest of her days with us filled with comfort, good food and a warm bed. She would have no part of my adoration. To the basement. Every once in a while she would call out to me and I would be permitted to tickle her belly. Not for long and don't be too rough Buster! After all, this is all my idea and it must be executed on my terms or else. I am just a visitor here and you had better learn early on, that it will be done my way! Ok then.

Paige likes to eat, that's for sure. Turkey, pizza, bologna, cheese, all the things a house cat should never munch on. Too bad! she would tell you with her insistence. I want that stuff and I am relentless in my approach. Well then, since she is so street wise and tough, I guess it won't hurt her, will it? Nope!

Well, earlier this year she showed signs of slowing down. Getting old I told myself, these things happen. She can't eat like she used to. She's not really herself and what in the world is going to become of her. After all, she has been a terrific pet and we have to do right by her. Off to the vet only to find out the eating problem was due to a tumour that would eventually take her life. We had the option to put her down right there and then. Nope! Let's bring the resilient feline home, we'll know when it is time.

Time went by. Paige healed as best she could. Look for excessive drooling and mood changes, the vet told us. Well that's exactly what we witnessed. After a while, she was not eating like she should, getting weaker by the day and then the harsh realization that now might be the time we dreaded. So, what to do!

Today was the day. I took on the task at hand while my wife was at work. Softly and gently, she left me. I stood there thinking about the last nine years and how they impacted us. She was just a pet, I thought to myself, or was she? Perhaps the tears on my keyboard may tell you a different story. Goodbye my precious girl, thanks for everything, I love you!

On a hill far away

I am reminded of a true story that helped put things in perspective for me.

A very old woman lay dying in a Halifax nursing home. Her devoted son sitting at her bedside was aware that his mother's time was near. "Don't forget" she reminded him, "where I am to be buried."

Now Mom, don't think about all that. Just rest.

"Promise me, that I will be buried where we talked about."

Yes Mother.

One sunny June afternoon a funeral filled with friends and family took place in the historic graveyard in Halifax. The sun shining through the trees reflected on some of the other headstones in the beautifully manicured cemetery. Sonny stood with his wife and all the old people and said goodbye to his loving mother. As an only child, he felt a special connection to his mother and to his father who had passed on before them.

It was not until the fall of that year that he went through her papers and got the shock of his life. Several shocks actually. First of all, he was not her only child, he was in fact, her thirteenth... His Dad, the only father he had ever known was not his biological father.

On December 6th, 1917 a knock came on her door. A neighbour stood there with some news. It seems there were two ships collided in the harbour, one of them was on fire, and it looked like they were gonna blow.

She instructed her family and husband to stay put, and to finish their breakfast before heading out the door for school. She would check this all out.

Just as she got close to the water, BOOM! The Halifax Explosion! 1500 metric tons of TNT blew everything to bits, turning the city and her people upside down. The force of the blast was so powerful that all of the water was blown out of the harbour. It was the first time man clearly saw the ocean floor. The chemical reaction filling the sky with poisonous gas caused a major blizzard crippling the already devastated city.

If you were not killed by the explosion, then you likely drowned by being pulled into the harbour by receding waters. If not, then you likely were frozen to death in the snowstorm. By some miracle she survived, pulled to safety by a man whose fate was similar. He lost everything as well.

In keeping with the times and wanting to do the right thing, he married the pregnant woman and together they built a new life. All of the people of Halifax gathered their dead and dying, and began to rebuild their lives. Help came from all over.

Quite often when a person suffers a trauma such as this one, the do not speak about it. Imagine her life as she once knew it was gone. Twelve children and their father wiped out in a single minute. She did her best to deal with the emotional, physical and financial situation at hand and the new baby in her arms.

This many years later all was revealed to the son. At his wife's urging he went to his mother's grave to talk to her. Of course he had many questions and rightfully so. It was then that his wife noticed that in the small hill just beyond her grave were twelve little foot stones glistening in the sun. She was reunited with her children so many years later.....

my point, if she never gave up and kept marching....why wouldn't I?

Of mice and menopause

One very important thing is that if girls act like ladies, it forces guys to act like gentlemen.

Growing up amidst the women I have, I am no stranger to the waves that emotions travel in and especially those filled with hormones. I have learned to endure if nothing else.

My guy friends, otherwise known as *the boys,* often tell me they have little or no understanding of their women. Good luck with that one. I offer the following. We, the male population are one way and the women are the other. We were raised differently, treated differently and expected to act differently and then we are thrown together and expected to make a life together. Sometimes it works and other times, not.

So here is what is wrong with the world. Men no longer have to go to war. As a result we don't do well with conflict and we are not appreciative of all we have, instead we are preoccupied with what we do not have.. People are critical now of things that were so very important to the world. Like religion for instance, a lot of people will tell you that they do not believe that God exists and if HE does the please prove it. It is not about proof, it is about believing in something higher than ourselves.

As far as I am concerned HE does exist. Had there not been a God, I would never have been given the beautiful mother I was. Had my father lived and our Mother died, heaven help us all. His first instinct (and men like him) would have been to go out and find us another mother. Pity help him with that one and pity help that poor woman whoever she is, we surely would've tied the pair of them up and left them at the end of the driveway. But God, in his infinite wisdom gave us our mother who in this boy's eyes was a Giant of a Woman who took on the task at hand and marched forward doing what she had to so her family was fed, quite often doing without for herself.

HE has also saved my sorry butt on many occasions, too many really but that is another story.

Then there is Sunday dinners at Grandma's. I think Sunday really should be a day of rest, the stores and businesses should be closed and people should spend Sunday dinner at the supper table. Phones set aside, and that goes for all devices and visit with your family. If it not your favorite thing to do then be 'glad' because it is seven whole days until you have to do it again. Communication is lacking in society to such a degree that I worry for future generations. Slow down, if even for a minute, regroup and then get going again.

Romance, courting and quality time is lacking in relationships. People rush into situations and don't take the time to get to know their partner. There is no other way to say it but to look at the big picture. Is this person respecting you and you them. Are they putting your feelings, needs and desires ahead of their own? Is it making you feel complete in their presence? If the answer is no to any of these then why put yourself through the torture, you cannot change another human being (unless they want to change). Oh don't get me wrong. Even the hardest of criminals can be tamed by the love of a good woman but if he ain't into to you, you are surely wasting your time.

The boys want a whore in the bedroom and a saint at the breakfast table. Yup and we want all kinds of acrobatics in the bedroom. We think about sex twenty-four-seven and hope you do too. We all secretly want a threesome and would love to do your best friend (without any repercussions of course) If given the chance would drink to excess, overindulge on fatty foods, never pick up after ourselves, sleep until noon, play video games or watch movies well into the night, begin and end the day with sex and that is all just this past weekend. But, truth be told we would never accomplish anything if we did not have the love, support and guidance of a good woman. Why? Because she brings sense and order to a crazy and cluttered world. The right woman will know when to rein you in and when to let you run. All this and menopause too!

So boys, learn to live with the heat flashes, mood swings, irritable days and loving moments because somewhere in that huge ball of estrogen is your life saver and someone who will take care of your sorry ass when you are unable to do so yourself. So make it easier on the both of you and cooperate, agree to disagree and life will run smoothly or at least I hope so. He he.

Jacqueline:
(an acknowledgment)

The first day I started in your restaurant I must tell you that I was fascinated with the dynamics that made up what proved to be an empire. Becky entered the walk in fridge only to have CJ close the door and subsequently place a screwdriver in the handle so she couldn't get out. I thought I might have to be a witness in an attempted murder trail but as it turned out they were boyfriend and girlfriend.

I was handed a set of keys and was told to unlock the front and side entrance doors. Well now, it seems that I had to insert the key in the bottom of the handle and twist. Honestly I had never seen anything like it. At first I thought it was a joke. As it turned out it was not a joke and it only took me six months to properly unlock those complicated doors.

I was reminded of growing up in my own family business when I saw several members of your family working in this very busy and productive food establishment. Like my own family the men were outnumbered by women, there were conflicts, struggles for attention and acceptance, competition, tears and laughter. There behind the counter was Big John, a gentle giant, a kind and humorous man who referred to CJ and Terry as don-kays.........it seems he might have been right.

I also had to learn the lingo, I never knew what the "new side" was nor "the pit" and was taken aback the first time when you asked CJ what he had in his drawers.....referring of course to how much was in the chicken drawers.

Despite the fact that I brought with me a reasonable amount of experience, I was quickly reminded that I was to forget all I learned in the past and re-learn your way of doing things. I did it. I kept an open mind toward all things and made the best of every situation. In doing so I feel that I began to grow. For that I am grateful.

On my first day you coined the phrase "A good server can make up for bad food but good food cannot make up for bad service." I never forgot it. It has helped me on so many levels as a server.

I brought with me my way with the public, a large following of customers, my sense of humour, my philosophies and my sarcasm. I felt welcomed into the fold by most people there and there were others I knew I had to win over. Some I did, some I didn't, and such is life.

Then, there before me was an unforgettable and overwhelming moment. From behind the office door, I could hear a screeching roar of a woman's voice one minute and then a hearty cackle of laughter the next. If I dare say so, it sent chills up my spine and might very well frizzle the mane of a wild beast. It was when the office door opened and Hurricane Jackie blew up the hall that was my first introduction as to how strong and powerful a presence you are. It was easy to see that you were the one in charge and this was your show all the way.

Over the years I grew to admire your resilience, tenacity, determination, business sense, organizational skills and your personality. None of this compared to the depth of the love that you have for your family. I also found out that you possessed outspoken opinions on every aspect of life and love. It is your delivery that might very well be too much for the average person. To them my advice has always been to hide under table 19 until it blows over.

Your standards in business are very high and I learned early on to work hard to get the job done, and do it correctly. I even learned how to sweep. You claimed once that "guys" never know how to sweep a floor properly. I was quick to say in our defense that 'we don't sweep the floor with our penises"....to which you quickly retorted "well it sure looks like you do.........."

It is now six years that I have been on your payroll, I have watched your ever expanding family grow and change. I see the stress on your face, in your voice and even in your actions. You really are the Queen of this dynasty. Your family is your creation and is your life's passion. I feel that you are at your best when you are surrounded by family and I also think you are at your most frustrated at the same time. I bet if someone asked you who in your family is your favorite, your answer might be, "The one who needs me the most at the moment...."

I have seen you in both harmony and conflict. Not with just your family but with all of us. We have all felt your wrath at one time or another. I have seen you nurse the ill, holler at the selfish, defend the innocent and crucify anyone of them brave enough to cross you (and that was all just yesterday).

You are a force to be reckoned with, a maverick of epic proportion and a crusader for the underdog.

So, having said all that, on the days when I don't feel like choking you, or walking out the door or even burning the restaurant down, I am sincerely grateful for your support during the most trying two years of my adult life. For all of this and then some, a sincere thank you for allowing me the chance to pick up the pieces of my life and put them back together.

P.S. Can I have a raise?

I'm Hungry!

Of all the things I talk and write about I am sure that food is the my favorite. I like to eat!

I was hungry as a child. Okay, we were not starving or anything like that but it sure felt like it. There were so many mouths to feed and all of us have hearty appetites so if you wanted it, you had better get it quick or it would be gone. Anyone from a large family knows exactly what I am talking about.

For the past 12 years or so I have attempted to write a cook book. This is at the urging of my friends and family who think I am fabulous in the kitchen. Writing that book is more difficult than even I could ever imagine. But I will share a few tips on this page. For instance, for a moister cake add moisture. I often add a 1/4 cup of apple sauce to my batter and the cakes come out moist. Some can say they can taste the apple sauce but I highly doubt it. That's because I have substituted yogurt the next time as I was out of apple sauce and yet they could still taste it. Go figure. The truth is a moist batter quite often results in a moist cake.

I love food and there is not much out there I do not like. I am a meat and potatoes guy but I will eat pizza, fish & chips, Chinese or Italian.... or a burger and fries, let's start with that. Do you use real hamburger for your BBQ? I do and I throw it in a bowl with bread crumbs, garlic powder, an egg, spices (even onion soup mix) a little Italian seasoning and then make them into patties. Yum! Sometimes I roll them in shake and bake for extra flavour. I slather my burgers with bbq sauce just as they about to finish on the grill. We all had to learn the hard way I am sure, not to put your sauce on the cooking meat until it is just about done as it will burn. Also just to add to your meal, do not forget your sauteed mushrooms and onions. Salt and pepper them but also add a drizzle of french dressing, it is another way that adds a flavour that no one can detect. They just look at you and say "this is delicious" and have little or no idea why.

Even if you don't eat your hamburger pattys on a bun you can have a couple on a plate (with melted cheese of course) along side your potato salad. This is a fav of mine made with real mayo as opposed to Miracle whip. Not that I don't add some to my mixture, I just prefer the flavour of the real stuff. I also add a drop of mustard to my potatoes, raw onion, a dribble of coleslaw dressing for that added zing. Yum, I am making my own mouth water. Then don't forget fresh bread rolls on the side.

When making pizza and rolling out your own dough, paint it with garlic butter before you place anything else on it, trust me on this one....delicious. Cook any hamburger or raw meats before putting them on a pizza, this cuts down on cooking time and food poisoning.

The best fruity summer and healthy drink is one can of pineapple juice, one can of apple juice and one can of orange juice. Mix them all up together. There is only one word to describe it, refreshing. This was a punch recipe I stumbled upon and you were to add pop and liquor to it. I left those two out and it became a healthy breakfast drink, it still is.

I love eggs and boiled eggs are just about my favorite. They are good hot and cold. Quite often I eat them in a salad but more importantly they need to be cooked right. Start out with eggs covered in cold water, add a dash of salt and a tsp of vinegar and bring to a boil in a pot with a tight fitting lid. Let them sit and the rest will take care of itself in six to ten minutes without removing the lid. It makes them easy to peel.

I love a sir fry as I am a connoisseur of all vegetables. You can use teriyaki sauce for flavor or soya or even Italian dressing, it adds a zing. Serve it over rice or noodles. When serving a garden salad add green onions and boiled eggs and then serve French dressing drizzled over it. You cannot beat the combination of flavours.

I always was a fan of lasagna but not of cottage cheese so my wife would take the cottage cheese and put it in the mixer, whip it into shape, it then becoming sour cream and it can be used all through the lasagna making it creamy and without the gritty texture of the cottage cheese. Ingenious? you bet.

There is a right and a wrong way to cook everything. Overcooking can be just as bad as under cooking anything. Follow directions and recipes to the 't'. try recipes out on friends and relatives not on company just in case it isn't up to par. When tackling a huge meal like a Roast Turkey Dinner with all the fixin', peel veggies the day before and soak them in cold water in the fridge and when cooking them, time them. There is nothing worse than having your potatoes done before your turnip and carrots. That's how twice cooked potatoes was invented. They are always done first so someone took them added sour cream, whipped them with butter and placed them in a casserole dish and baked them for fifteen minutes before serving. Yum, OK, double yum.

Don't forget to save your broth for gravy. Place it in dishes to freeze. During this process the fat will rise to the top and you can toss it, there you go, guilt free gravy broth. For those of you who are gluten free thicken your gravy with corn starch rather than flour. And then there is the stuffing. Lots of people make homemade dressing, you know the one with a large amount of potato to the bread, onions and summer savory. I do more of a stuffing with bread and eggs, sausage meat, onions, celery, potatoes, sage and summer savory...yup, the best part of the meal. And these are all carbs so be sure and take a nap afterward.

When roasting a turkey everyone has a preference. I use a roaster with a tight fitting lid. (It keeps the moisture inside). Cook it on medium heat. Others cook theirs face down, uncovered, on low heat, on high heat, with stuffing inside of it and others not. I think you should add a handful of celery to the inside of the bird (for moisture), garlic and butter on the outside and a strip or two of bacon to add a bit of flavor to the bird but definitely to the broth. It makes fabulous gravy.

Walk the Dog

When my dog took seriously ill I was told that "Twelve years is long enough for any dog so you might consider putting her down" I disagreed on so many levels. All of us have heard tales of dogs living to be 18 years old or even twenty. I wasn't ready to give up on her, she was all I had.

Newly separated and after having been through an emotional crisis, I leaned on her for support more than ever. She became the reason I got up in the morning. So, I looked for ways to better care for her. I researched meds and went a holistic route and even followed the advice of an animal psychic. All seems to work and we continue to do so some two and a half years later. The girl is in amazing good health.

Am I grateful? Yes, Am I realistic when it comes to her time here on earth? Absolutely. But, I was not ready to give up on her nor was I ready for her to give up on herself. So we did something that we had not practiced for a number of years, we walked. I dug out her leash and collar and every morning and every night out we went. I don't particularly like walking as she is a small dog and takes small steps. I am a big guy and I take large strides, however, we met in the middle. I was able to see the positive effects on her and that made me feel better. Also, it never occurred to me that the walks were doing something good for me as well. Perhaps I needed to take my mind off my troubles for a minute and during these moments was able to do just that.

When we returned from these bonding moments the dog as not only exercised, she was tired and a good kind of tired. I always felt guilty about keeping her inside while I was at work as she played very little so I often pictured her sitting alone and waiting for her Daddy to come home. Man, I do not know how parents do it. My favorite singer Anne Murray often spoke in interviews about how guilty she felt leaving her kids even though they were in good hands. I can see it.

So it was up to me to make the most of our time together and to be productive, that mostly being my including her in all I did. Car rides are great for dogs like her as you can take them anywhere with little or no fuss. The deck is her second home during the summer months and she loves a warm breeze and fresh air, then it's nap time with daddy. She is undoubtedly my companion.

Now, what am I going to do when the end comes? First of all, I am going to cry. I know that because I cry now if I think about it too much but I am not an idiot. I know that nothing lasts forever, so what's a man to do? Well, glad you asked. I live everyday like it's our last. I love her, talk to her, walk her, cuddle her, brush her and take care of her. I have rearranged my schedule, my routines and my life for her. Her needs come before my own. This way I know I can go to work and not worry about her (well not too much). My neighbors have permission to kick my door in in case of fire and even if you don't have my number, everyone knows where I work so they CAN get a hold of me if need be.

I make sure she get the proper health care she needs no matter what the cost and the same goes for her grooming. I had her all dolled up this week but came up a little short on my own haircut. Oh well. All because that scrunchy little face has eyes that love me and only me.

She is my baby and I am her Daddy.

I love you Rozie!

My Grandmother's Kitchen

When my grandmother was in her late seventies she began to show signs of decline and why wouldn't she? She worked hard all her life. While this is not unusual, it wasn't easy for us as a family to witness. I was eight years old when I really took notice of what a wonderful woman she really was. Funny and entertaining, she always had an interesting story to tell.

Her place was in the kitchen. There in her cupboards were neatly arranged rows of tea cups and saucers. In a drawer were perfectly folded tea towels and dish clothes, some of them twenty or so years old. A place for everything and everything in it's place. In the brightly lit corner of the kitchen near a window, was her sewing area. On the tiny table were her glasses and next to them, her bible. Some days were filled with sewing and others reading the written word. She found comfort in both.

On her stove was a continuous full pot of steeped tea. "That reminds me," she said out loud. "Goodwin's's has tea on sale today, I must get Papa some". Then, a little embarrassed, she realized that Papa was not with us anymore. She looked down into my face and said. "I'm so used to having him around, that I forget that he's gone." I knew she wanted to cry but what good would that do? Back to her cooking.

Our grandmother was good at everything she did. Her house was always neat and tidy, her back yard neatly manicured and her life itself was orderly and old fashioned. It was however, her cooking skills that were the envy of the neighborhood. There was no longer any reason to open her cookbooks as she had mastered all of the recipes. Anything from a simple meatloaf to a full Roasted turkey dinner with all of the trimmings, each and every meal was a masterpiece.

Through the window you could see how healthy her garden was. This year we had the perfect amount of rain so everything was coming along nicely. As she looked out she thought to herself. I wonder if this is the last year I will spend in this house. Since Papa had died the year before, she was lonely, not sad. She busied herself with cooking for the neighbors or for fund raiser for the church. Homemade pickles and preserves, jams and jellies and of course, her famous fruitcakes.

When our sister married an Acadian, she whipped up a pot of pea soup. While a few in the family turned their nose up at such a delicacy, most thoroughly enjoyed it. He especially enjoyed the friendly gesture an asked her if she would like to adopt him as her grandchild. "I already did" was her reply.

On the day she died it was like any other June day, a soft breeze blowing across a cluster of mayflowers that had bloomed in the morning sun.. Wheat toast for breakfast, a hot cup of tea to go along with it, biscuits in the oven. As she stood to check on her cooking, the angels swept in and in a moment she softly floated to the floor. Never one for much fanfare nor a burden to anyone, she left the world the same way she entered it, quietly, taking our hearts with her.

Shelly: Gee, I am Sorry!

Living in, and growing up with the snotty people I did, in the town of Amherst, was to say the least, challenging. I did not have much going for me in the fitting in quality. I wasn't an athlete, I wasn't a scholar, and I wasn't a millionaire. I was just a poor boy from the wrong side of the tracks.

My father died when I was in grade six and that left an empty void in my life. Even though I grew up in a picturesque neighborhood, and had lots of kids to interact with, I was a lonely and sad kid, an outcast. I survived despite my short-comings. Like most teens, I was emotionally wrapped up in my distaste for life. My best friend was Brian Ripley, my closest friend was another Brian, an adopted boy. I so envied his hockey skills, his popularity, and his having any other family but his own. My emotions and loneliness may have run a bit deeper than his did but still I envied him, he had an escape. He had another mysterious family somewhere.

I was forced against my will to attend senior high, otherwise known as Amherst Regional High School. I hated every moment of it! Okay, there were a few bright moments, the way Mrs. Pipes made me feel important and then there was Mr. Angel and his choice of songs for the music class, but there was little else.

I did not like school, I did not like the long walk to school, and I did not like having to force myself into entering the building on any level. Those were really not my people. Get it?

It was a building full of misfits, jocks, dead-heads, druggies, losers and me. How we all survived, I will never know. It probably due to the fact that I met decent friends like Brian, Duncan, and Kevin that got me through the rough times.

And then it is a coming of age moment for me, a truly eye opening experience. A crazy girl from just outside of town, someone who today might have been diagnosed as bi-polar, was picked on, no I should say, she was harassed, or should I say, she was targeted. Shelly G. was a nervous and emotional girl who, looking back now, was kicked while she was down. It got to the point that she was crying every day. I never cried, so I had no sympathy for someone so emotionally unstable. Kids pounced on her weakness. She was harassed in the halls and picked on in the stairwell, so much so, that one evil day someone pulled her by the book bag and caused her to fall down the stairs backwards, head over heels. I saw her lying at the bottom of the stairs, crying.

It occurred to me than that I was the worst one there. Oh, I wasn't the one who caused that girl to fall, but I was the one who said nothing. I did nothing. That made me the worst of all. To this day that very act of cruelty has haunted me. I was the one that did not speak up, I was the one that allowed another human being to be treated like dirt and for what, so someone who had more going for them than she did, would feel superior to her, and to us, and to the world? I think not!

Shelly G., wherever you are, take my word as a man, from this day forward, I, Todd Canton, stand up for those individuals who, for whatever reason, decide to prove themselves different, so that every person, no matter who they are, or where they come from, that they all, and I mean all, have the chance to experience life in a safe and friendly environment with at least one individual who will speak up when I see an injustice, and because of you, I am not afraid to do so.

God Bless You Shelly G., wherever you are.

Winter Meeting

Our pastures were lightly covered with snow. That is always a good thing. It's December and this is the time for snow. Since global warming is upon us, I feel much better when we have seasonal and predictable weather when we are supposed to. It's easier on my pets too. The horses consume hay and are happy to be in the warmth of the barns. I enjoy the walk to the barns in the morning. So does my dog, Bentley. She is a collie mix and is the most faithful companion a man could ask for.

Moving to a farm was the smartest thing my wife and I have ever done. The horses aren't ours. We allow the neighbor to use the facilities at his own risk. I much prefer chickens and ducks, and the wild deer that feed on the perimeter of our property. I built the hen house myself, I even assisted in building suitable quarters for our ducks alongside the pond in our back yard. It really makes it beautiful. As winter settles in the chickens stay inside and get plump. Not only do they supply us with fresh eggs but they are sometimes, our main course. I cannot kill a chicken myself and I refuse to eat duck. I am too tender-hearted to do the killing but I do enjoy eating part. That goes for the beef too. My neighbor John Morgan always fills our freezer with freshly cut roasts and we enjoy them thoroughly.

The reason I live on a farm is to lower my stress level. It was either that or die, my doctor informed me. So I listened. I love chickens and view them more as pets than I do a farm animal. I just want them taken care of. The ducks are for a selfish reason. I fell in love with waterfowl as a boy and since then, I simply enjoy watching them and listening to them chat the day away. They are in their own little world and I do my best to keep them safe from any predators.

Up behind the barns, my wife and I each have a garden. In the summer months I grow vegetables and she grows flowers. Both are beautiful and cultivated. Mine is fenced in so the wild deer and jack rabbits don't eat all I've grown, and she has carefully crafted a fence for all her colorful and pretty flowers to embrace.

After working in business for so long I didn't think I would like all the quiet but I have adapted nicely. The air is clean and fresh and so is our life out here. It's the walks I take around the wooded property that fascinates me the most. To see wildlife in it's natural habitat in whatever form, is heartwarming.

There is a tall, old, wooden fence that separates our acreage from our neighbors, and it stands strong. All along the fence the view is beautiful. Quite often in the Spring you will see a doe or two with a fawn. I thought the fence was to divide our properties, but later, I find out it was to keep the deer at a respectful distance. They really are beautiful creatures and as long as I knew the boundaries, I was able to view them without threat of interference on my part.

One doe in particular caught the scent of mine in the wind and that will usually cause the group to disperse. She seemed comfortable in my presence. Perhaps she had contact with man on a friendly basis over the course of time and felt unthreatened. I probably shouldn't do it but I often find myself bring carrot greens and apples to the fence and with my strongest arm, throwing them over. I know the deer enjoys this because I think they look for me. My newest friend, Sophie, comes the closest to the fence. She is like the lookout. Once she says it's okay, then it's a go for the rest.

There is something special about Sophie. She 's gentler than the others and more trusting too. This could be a dangerous thing for all of us. That's why I try to keep a respectful distance. She does come close enough that I can see how pretty her eyes are. Eyes are the mirror to the soul, isn't that what they say? She looks at me tenderly and sometimes tilts her head in amazement, the whole time on the alert for noises in front and back of her.

Yesterday she didn't show. In fact none of them walked along the fence wall. It was a reasonable day and for the life of me, I could not imagine what was going on. After a day or two things were back to normal. When I mentioned to John Morgan the mysterious events, he told me one of them must've given birth, and without Sophie, none would be allowed to leave the herd. All would form a circle around the doe and fawn until it was up and running. How magnificent I thought this was, a real miracle. John Morgan was right. There in the middle of the herd, a young doe had her fawn ever so near. Sophie, for the first time approached the fence. Standing inches from me, I could see her breath in the cool morning air, and had the chance to look into those beautiful eyes. From my hand I offered her a large carrot with a huge green top. Gently she took it from me and walked over and placed it at the feet of the young mother.

My heart was pounding so loud I could hear it in my ears. She really was the matriarch of the group. I think this little fawn was her grand-daughter and she brought them out to see me. I was never so humble in business as I was in the beauty of my own back yard.

Nature is wondrous, life is beautiful.

frEaK

Growing up in the town I did and with the people I did, I can't say it was all roses and sunshine. It had its moments but I didn't get to be who I am today without jumping at least a few hurdles. In the elementary school that I attended, I was able to successfully fill the shoes of my older siblings and to carry on the tradition of being, well, average. It was the year I attended grade six that was my defining moment as a human being.

There was a boy in the other grade six class who was a freak. He had an artificial arm. As far as I knew he couldn't talk normally or anything like that. As far as I knew he was what they all called him, a freak. In an effort to grow socially it was decided that the two grade six classes would combine for such subjects as music, art and gym. I hated all of these classes, mostly because I had no talent. I couldn't play any kind of instrument, couldn't draw anything worthwhile and I defiantly sucked at any kind of physical activities. The reason I say it that way was I never even gave it a chance so how could I know. I was, after all, my own worst enemy. Then we had to choose teams. Do you know where I am going with this? Yup! I was chosen last. What a great feeling that is. At least the freak was worse than me, but not by mush.

BJ made sure that I knew I was chosen last. There he was a good athlete, handsome and popular and always had money on him. We were lucky to have a nickel to spend on candy at Fred's store but BJ always seemed to have a 20$ bill. This he flaunted in front of us as well as the fact that I was chosen last. Although it was fast becoming, me and the fREaK, that were chosen last.

So there we are, sitting on the bench side by side, me and Arthur Edward Prendergast III, or ARTIE as his freakish family called him. Well too bad for you, I thought to myself, I am not going to play with you. One thing I did master over the years was sulking. I could do it for hours. All I had to do was concentrate on the one thing that didn't ever let me down, me. I simply would shut off the rest of the world and that was that. Nothing and I mean nothing, not a teacher or a friend could penetrate the stone wall that I had built around me. "If you play doubles with me against BJ in volleyball I will treat you at the dairy Queen." he suggested. "Huh?" I thought to myself. "What?' he repeated this offer and I simply could not refuse. After all, volleyball is not that hard and Dairy Queen, well there is nothing like it. Banana milkshakes and brazier burgers.

Over he goes to BJ and although I can't hear the conversation, I think I knew it's contents. Back he comes with BJ and one of his cronies. We begin. Well, I have certainly learned a lot in my life but not as much as I did that day. First off, a prosthetic arm can hit a volley ball with amazing power, a freak from the wrong side of the tracks has hidden talents and three, never to pass up a chance to go to the Dairy Queen. As we walked down the long hill and up the road toward town I got to know Arthur Edward Prendergast III, not as a disabled person, but as a human being. There was a heart beating in his chest, and a bright mind at work all the time. He was a human being after all. We talked about the hideous arm with the forceps at the end, and how he fell in front of the lawn mower when his grandfather was mowing the lawn. He also told me about how the doctor told his mother he would be better off in a special school within an asylum with others like *him* and how she refused to see him as anything but her little boy. You can imagine my surprise when he paid with BJ's crisp 20$ bill.

It just goes to show folks, God doesn't make mistakes, people do.

Arthur is now a savvy business man who lives near Saint John and produces prosthetic limbs for children that are so real hardly anyone could tell the difference. I believe he is a millionaire, I can only wonder what BJ is doing today and me, well I'm just me.

Onward and Upward

No matter what happens to you and no matter how many times you get knocked down, get up again. Easier said than done, but it *can* be done. I heard a phrase once that went something like this, "No man ever drowned because he fell in the river, he drowned because he didn't fight hard enough to get out". Although it's harsh, there is some truth to it. If you give up then the waters win. So a man has to fight continually for his life.

While some people appear to have a fantastic life filled with good fortune and happiness, they don't. They just make the most of what they have. Death come to every person's life and so does sickness and tragedy. How you handle it and how you wear it is up to you. I was told as a kid that life is like climbing a mountain and after that mountain is another and another, so get climbing. After you climb so high it might not be a good idea to look down or even over your shoulder. At least not until you are definitely over the worst of the climb. Make sense? So if you want to sit and lament about your life and the mountains you have to climb, then you may very well find yourself sitting alone. No one will listen and ever be envious or jealous of you.

As a server I tend to get sore legs and often utter the words "I'm getting too old for this." but really I am not. I am just tired so I looked into vitamins to help replenish my ageing body. I take walks in the warm and cool weather. I also found shoes that support feet and legs, what a difference it has made. I now feel that I can tackle anything. All of this happened because I refused to give in or give up. If I can't walk through a problem, I tend to find a way around it. Onward and Upward.

Same goes for a lot in my life. Now don't think for a moment that I don't get discouraged and frustrated. I do. But, I make an honest effort for it not to take over me. This is where living in the moment makes all the difference. A man can go to bed tired from a good day's work or exhausted from doing nothing. Choose. I make sure I get a good night's rest so I can tackle what the next day offers and when I look at the pile of work ahead of me, I dig in. As we all know work doesn't do itself so if I set out to build a brick wall, it all starts with picking up that first brick. Then one by one it begins to fall into place. Pretty soon, brick by brick, you have a whole wall and a strong one.

Living in the moment has become my new path to follow in life. If I look too far ahead on my work schedule, I get myself tired. So I look at it this way. Let's face today and look forward to tomorrow, we'll take care of the rest later. Concentrate on the task at hand and only that, why over work your brain about something you cannot control today. It really does make sense when you think about it. I make sure that I am reminded how lucky I am that I can work. I probably will work until I die, as I feel being productive is very important to my well being. And a man can only take charge of his life with a proper attitude. Allowing discouragement or despair into your every day life can bring you down. Do not be jealous of others but set your goals to achieve greatness in your own life. Make up your mind to achieve what you feel is important. Do remember though, a lot of people get along and are happier with less than what you and I have.

Either I am making sense on these pages or I am confirming that I am full of sh!t!

The Wisest Words I Have Ever Heard!

Calling Someone else Ugly does not make you any more Beautiful

Ain't that the truth! Our mother was a sharp woman with a deeply rooted intelligence, and she was a survivor. She taught us all to see the beauty in everything, that there really was a silver lining and as bad as things are, they could certainly be worse. She also taught us that if you look for the good in people you will surely find it.

Stop complaining about your life when so many others are fighting for theirs!

I am such a whiner when it comes to getting out of bed in the morning so every once in a while I am reminded that I am a lucky man when my feet hit the floor in the mornings. Some guys a lot younger than me may never get out of their bed again. So if you are fortunate enough to be able to do so then do so. My friend Irene once told me that a person can be glad they put on their own shoes in the morning because someone else might be taking them off that night. Like the funeral directer.

The definition of true friendship is despite the fact that you may disagree, you look down and you are still holding hands.

Every one of us has had a friend at one time or another that stopped being our friend because we disagreed. In that case you have to wonder if that was a real friendship or not. But, we also have that person that keeps coming back, accepts you for the misfit you really are and likes you anyway.

If You Don't Like my Gate, then don't Swing on it!

Again our mother who seemed to have an answer for everything coined this phrase when someone constantly criticized her. It comes from the day when home and yards were quit often fenced in and a gate at the entrance for the post man. Most fences were so strong a kid or two could play on the gate and enjoy the simple pleasure of swinging on the gate.) She, our strong mother, was adamant about her life and how she ran it. So if you were bothered by it and offered no better way to do things then move along.

Appreciate your Parents while they are here as you will surely think about them when all that is left is an empty chair!

So many people complain about their parents but fall apart when something happens to them. Then of course, it's too late. You cannot take harsh words back, you can apologize but really once the damage is done, well you know the rest. So it would be wise to take a look

Life Doesn't Have to be Perfect to be Wonderful

around at all you have while you have it (and don't pay too much to all you don't!) One day them and those like them will all be gone and all we will have left are memories. Tears are made by memories and regret. That's what they meant in the Bible when they said to 'honor thy mother and thy father.'

If a man takes a chance, sometimes good things happen, sometimes bad things happen but if a man doesn't take a chance, nothing happens.

This is a great collection of wise words and some that people can live by. I would love to take the credit for them but alas it is from the Golden Girls. It reaches out to those too scared of life to live it. Get off that couch, go outside, see people and accept what the day brings. Know onw knows what's on the other side of the fence until they look. Correct?

I Overlooked an Orchid while searching for a Rose.

I am a lucky man, I love orchids. You see, I learned a long time ago that everything is beautiful and that an orchid can be just as beautiful in someone's eyes as a dozen roses. So many people pass by others thinking that what's (or who) is up the road is so much better. It is an ugly lesson to learn. Conway Twitty and his daughter Joni sang a song called *Don't Cry Joni* that spoke of this very subject. Or maybe you can search out the story Welcome to Holland. It is beautiful.

The Grass is Always Greener on the Other Side

probably speaking about pot! Ha ha......honestly if you do not know this one, you have a lot to learn.

Happy Wife, Happy Life

Speaks volumes that statement does. How many times have we been told that if Mama ain't happy, ain't nobody happy. Learn this one quick boys! The sooner the better.

Sometimes God removes People from your Life for a Reason, try to remember that before you go running after them...

I cannot tell you how many times I have witnessed this and how frustrating it can be. I have also been that person who did the running after. I guess I figured that if I was able to impress them then they might like me more. As it turned out they didn't and I have just made a complete fool of myself. Sometimes it's a hard lesson to learn but truly a valuable one.

On the other hand I have always been of the opinion that i was interesting ang certainly enough to entertain the masses. Now I realize that those who thought not are the real losers. Better to have loved and lost than not to have loved at all. Ha. Hurt feelings are hurt feelings. Live and learn might be a better way of putting it.

It is up to you to find the Beauty in the Ugliest of days!

It is very easy to get caught up in all the negativity that goes on in every day life so someone has to take the other path. Rainy days bring people down but let me tell you that it has been my experience that when you take a walk on a rainy evening with that somebody special it takes on a whole new perspective. Take that a little further, rain is a much needed part of our lives so let it do its job and nourish us. We will all be better for it.

So one day on my way somewhere, I ran out of gas (human error) I cannot help but be grateful that I have a car to take gas to and that despite it having cold seats, your bottom is safe inside when others are walking through life. Look up at the skies and take in all the beauty, just like there is massive beauty on snowy days and even windy ones. The world really is a majestic place, take a look around, and you will find the beauty in the ugliest of days. You might even find some beauty in the ugliest of people. Life doesn't have to be perfect to be wonderful.

Life Doesn't have to be Perfect to be Wonderful!

Not only is this a perfect title for my book but an appropriate title for my life and how I see it. Let's face it, considering the ugly spot my life was in what with my marriage breaking up, my financial situation and my being up on sex charges, holy cow! However, I got through it all. Am I bruised? yes, but beaten no! I continue to march forward and with a positive attitude, good intestinal fortitude and a stubborn streak a mile long, I thrive. I live in moments, not time and I make the most of these moments as they happen.

I Know Why the Caged Bird Sings! Is the title of one the many writings of Mayo Angelou, an astounding and prophetic woman who speaks to every suffering human being and we listen. For many years I could not imagine what a caged bird would ever have to sing about but then one day it occurred to me that it had food and water, shelter and security of sorts...but...it was still confined. Aren't we all? So, make the best of every situation despite any confinements and like that caged bird one day someone will leave the door open and you will have the opportunity to fly free if you so choose........

Don't be afraid of pressure. Remember that pressure is what turns a lump of coal into a diamond.

Too many times people lament about their struggles and I just shake my head. The is no life without struggles starting with birth when a baby less than ten pounds has to push its way out of its mother's body and into the world. Then you discover that crawling and walking has its share of bumps and bruises. Then we try to ride bikes, play sports, wrestle and take chances that could end up who knows how but somehow we make it through. Then we enter relationships, the work force and adulthood and all they have to offer. So, having said all of this, if we can make it this far then any pressure we are under, we can probably handle and prove ourselves to be the diamond underneath it all. True?

Sitting in church does not make you any more Saint than sitting in a garage makes you a car.

The world is full of hypocrites, they all have too much to say and let's face it, who wants to hear it? We already know we are not perfect, that we mess up and are all only human after all so why remind us. The truth is there are no perfect people on ly those that think they are and yet somehow we all know the difference. Also, we are kind enough that when one of those supposedly perfect people mess up, we don't mention it.

I'd rather be an hour early than a minute late.

This is true on so many levels but so much more so than in the food business. Those of us whose heart can be found smack in the middle of the hospitality business know that the earlier you begin your day the more you get done. Organization is the key word and efficiency is its twin brother. Early to bed and early to rise falls under the same category. Staying up all hours of the day and night doing heaven knows what and then dragging your butt around all day at work is of no value to anyone. Get some rest as tomorrow is coming whether you are prepared or not.

So as the organized and meticulous person I am, I insist on starting before I am supposed to and ending when the job is done to my satisfaction. Then I feel that I have accomplished something and all parties benefit.

Church is not a Gathering Place for Saints, it's a Hospital for Sinners.

This is similar to the previous status but just as important. It was either Ann Landers or her sister Abigail VanBuren who said it first and that was a while ago but it stuck with me. So many times others tend to look down their noses at others. The point being that just because you go to church, it does not mean that you are pure, but going there is a beginning to self discovery and the fact of just how pure you are not.

The two of them were not only wise but they had the snappiest of comebacks. Like for instance. "My boyfriend thinks all girls are the same, how can I show him different?" Take him to the beach. And "My sister insisted she got pregnant by sitting next to a boy at church" Well, somebody must've moved.

And then there is my own: After many corny jokes one of my co-workers stated "You are such a dick" to which I replied,

Yup, then stop jerking me around.

My co-worker told me she had the people at her table in the palm of her hands. I said the last thing I had in the palm of my hands spit all over me. I do not know exactly where this all comes from but mostly the comments pop out before I can even stop them.

Sugar Plums

When speaking about my mother I quite often start out by stating how terribly intelligent she was. I often get a doubtful look or two, but it is the truth. She was the smartest person I ever met in my life. She was smarter than I was and that is saying something as I was pretty slick as a child. It is said that I had the highest IQ at Amherst Regional High School, but unfortunately for me I was the laziest student there too.

As a young woman my mother was tall and slender with coal black hair. That is *not* the woman I remember. *My* mother was a tall, fat and prematurely gray woman, with a sharp wit, an immense and insightful personality and an amazing sense of humorous timing. Convinced? Born to an unwed mother of Chinese descent and given up for adoption, she learned right off the art of survivability. She was no quitter and was sensible enough to see the path before her and as a result made a lot of good choices.

She met and married our father in Amherst and they made a life together. It was a quiet and nice life until we, the kids, came along. First our sister Joan, then Edith, Jack, Susan and a few years later, Anne, Ruth and Todd. We all came with our own personalities and quirks and in doing so filled that house on Russell Street with music and laughter and love and war. Our mother became the center of our universe and so, from there on, all we experienced in the big world, we would run home to her, to share.

When our mother was forty-three years old, she found herself in a difficult situation. A mother of seven, she was also a widow. I don't know yet how she kept things together but she managed to keep an optimistic outlook on life. I often questioned her on this positive attitude. She said it went back to her days growing up in a coal mining family. Her father Dan Gillis was a miner like his father before him and they lived a coal miner's life. Despite the hardships that they faced every day, you still moved forward and the one thing you never did was give up.. This fiery sense of determination was passed onto all the Gillis children and as a result all seem to be upbeat and forward looking people despite the bleakest moments of their lives.

It was the first Christmas after our father had passed away that I was able to view the strength that my mother, as a woman, possessed. We were almost destitute financially but she was able to pull of a successful Christmas. Not just that year, but every year. Looking back it wasn't the toys, it was the tree. It wasn't the amount of gifts, it was the gift of life and laughter. It wasn't the turkey dinner as much as it was the gravy afforded, if you know what I mean?. It was the taste of fruitcakes that Mom's aunt Mary Soppa had fashioned with her own gentle hands. If I try to make a list of gifts that I received over the years I'm afraid it might be a short one. Spirograph, a record player and Annie, Anne Murray's sultry and soft LP.

I can however, tell you about the Christmas tree and how our mother always used too much garland. But my, how it sparkled in the evenings. Those evenings when we would sit and sing. I can recall the long table where she fashioned a Nativity scene above and a valley below filled with tiny houses and deer and sheep and cows. I can smell the scent of Red Rose tea steeping on the stove in the kitchen. I can recall blustery Amherst winters filled with snow blowing in from the Tantramar Marsh. I can remember anticipating our sister Edith's return from school in Cape Breton and the fear that we would not all be together if she wasn't there for the holidays, especially since it was the first one without Dad there.

I can remember making the most of our vacation from school by tobogganing down the hills overlooking the marsh. I can especially remember my father and how his memory has never left me. A vision of a quiet and gentle man sitting in the corner smoking an Export cigarette and reading the paper. But, I guess of all the visions of sugar plums that I carry in my heart, there is one above all. There in the very center of all that's Christmas and family and love, was my mother Vivian Canton, the very glue that held our family together..

Many years later our mother was diagnosed with ALS. She fought that disease the same way she tackled every other obstacle she faced in her life, with strength and determination. She fought to the very end. All I can say about the whole situation is that I wonder if it all happened for a reason. Perhaps to teach those around us that life really is precious and that we all should appreciate and enjoy *sugar plums* when they come our way.

The Thought of Anne

Our sister Anne was our mother and father's *love* child.

Now in some people's books that means our parents were not married. They were, but had suffered an interruption that might have spelled the end of them as they knew it. It brought them closer together than they had ever been after a few emotional setbacks. It may have had something to do with the fact that Mother nearly died giving birth to Anne, or the fact that Dad had finally found true love in the face of our mother. Either or, it happened. Both were quick to be reminded just how precious life is.

We, as a family, are not jealous of the fact that Anne was our mother's favorite. We all can see her special qualities. If any of us was having a knock down, drag 'em out fight, it was never with Anne. She was, if I dare say, the fawn of our family. A kind and gentle soul who devoted her life to one thing, loving our mother.

Mother never gave her things that she didn't give us, she never filled her bowl more than she did ours, it was more the fact that Anne seemed to appreciate our mother more than we did. When it came to Mother's Day or her birthday, Anne would find the tenderest card. The words on the page would tell our mother how much she loved her and those words were true. Anne's heart was always filled with thoughts of our mother. At least it sure looked that way.

Anne embarrasses easily. She is such a gentle and shy soul, one really doesn't want to offend her. If you did, your conscience would get the best of you. You really don't want to hurt Anne's feelings, that just wouldn't be right. Mother would be mad at you and the rest of us might very well pound you when we get you alone. "Leave her alone", we would say, "she never hurts anybody". And she didn't.

After school we would all run home so we could play. Our life was spent outside. Sledding, tobogganing, skating. Anne might very well sit inside and read her homework to Mother and talk to her about what kind of day she had. Mother always seemed to enjoy that.

Anne would stay by our mother's side when she was preparing supper. Always helpful, she did the best job that a daughter could do. This only deepened Mother's affection for Anne. Mother would often tell us about the day the doctor said that she might have to make a choice over her own life or that of her child. Our mother was quick to say "Save my child, my husband is a good man, he'll marry again." Our father, on the other hand, said, "Save my wife, I cannot raise six kids on my own." You know something? He would have resented Anne had she caused our mother's death. It's a good thing it worked out the way it did. I guess when he held her in his arms for the first time he told our mother. "This one is fragile," and she was. Fragile and strong at the same time. Like our mother, Anne survived against the odds.

This was proven all too recently when our mother was diagnosed with, and consequently died from ALS. Anne took care of her. She washed and brushed her hair, and changed her clothes. She sat up at night and talked to and read to our mother. Both Anne and our sister Ruth did such a grand job taking care of her that I find it very difficult to criticize either of them whenever they mess up, and let me tell you something folks, that's not very often.

We all kind of agree that Anne should have been a nurse. She has such a caring way about her. She never had any babies of her own but she had babies in other ways. They love her as much as she loves them. Love is what is in her heart. Our Anne's been a little lonely of late, Mother is gone, and she finds herself working all the time. Anne likes to keep busy, it takes her mind off things.

As far as this all goes, I just wanted to say: Anne, you've been on my mind lately, and I wanted to find a way to say..................thanks for making each and everyone of stop and smell the roses. It seems that you have become the rose in all of our lives.

just your brother,

Todd

Cryin' my Heart Out Over You...

I love country music but let me tell you something. When you suffer a breakup it seems that every song is about her. So on the days I am feeling sad out come the tunes. Some of them are poignant and some are down right heart wrenching. Same goes for pop music as well. Elton John wrote Sad Songs Say so Much and it is absolutely true. The Love Inside is a beautiful ballad by Barbra Streisand and The Colour of my Love by Celine Dion are two exquisite pieces of work.

Home by Blake Shelton or Michael Buble bring a tear to my eye and Carrie Underwood's performance of Randy Travis's I told You So is stunningly beautiful. Surprisingly, the words to Anne Murray's hit Snowbird are quite sad as well. Barbara Mandrell's Years is a beautiful ballad.

You do realize that I could go on forever but the point I want to make is every once a while you need a down day and maybe hear a sad or soft tune, followed by you crying your eyes out and when that's all over, get back up and keep marching. Never let the blues take over you.

I haven't cried in years. Truly. When I do it usually involves an animal being hurt or injured or killed. My heart i so tender when it comes to the animal kingdom that I suspect it will be my downfall in the end.

I believe that love is the foundation of our very being and if you are not capable of giving and receiving love, then you surely have a problem or two on your hands. A child needs love and affection to prosper, we as adults require the same in finding a life's partner. It makes for a more pleasant life if it is governed by love. Not just for each other but for life itself, the world we live in and the people that we co-exist with.

I must tell you that I am one of the lucky ones. I learned early on what true love is and it has helped make me a better man. I did however have to be taught a few things, like empathy and compassion. My college professor Hugh MacIntyre taught me empathy and my mother taught me compassion. I was born with neither. I simply looked at the world in a black and white manner, others showed me the color of life and the color of love.

My mother told me that all living things had feelings and I should always remember that statement. I do. Once I cornered a mouse and it surely knew its fate. But as I looked into those beady little eyes, I thought to myself; how many times have I been backed into a corner? I certainly didn't like the feeling and I suspect that little critter didn't either. So I used a broom to guide him out of the situation and gave him one chance to run, and he did.

Hugh told me that I was the most intuitive person he had ever met and that when he got through with me I would be able to sit in a room with an abused child and the abuser and not pass judgment. Well! It took a lot of work on his part but by GOD I did it. He drilled it into my brain that long before I came riding in on a white horse, they were a family, and they will remain one long after I am gone. Ok then.

So having said all of this how can you not think me to be a complicated human being.

Every Kick is a Boost!

How many times have you said to yourself, that guy need a kick in the ass. Sometimes a kick and a swift one at that seems to be exactly what some people need to shock them into reality and to get them moving. I have on occasion, seen it make the biggest difference in the world and I have also seen it make that receiver dig their heels in all the more. Every action has a reaction.

It seems we live in a world where one is constantly being put down for one thing or another. Sad but true. Our mother always said, *don't ever think you can build yourself up by putting others down.* I never forgot that. I try never to criticize anyone unless I feel they deserve it.

What I did learn along the way is that you will take your fair share of kicks from other people be they jealous, hateful or just plain nasty. How you react to all of that is entirely up to you. Never give anyone else the power over your life. You only have one life to live, take the bull by the horns and in doing so make the most of your life.

Now with some put downs you have to decide if it is your pride that is hurt or your feelings or you. Then retaliate. Is their merit to the kick or does it make you more determined than ever to overcome any of the pain or hurt it has caused. It is a case of making something positive out of any negative vibes that come your way. It can be done.

Every kick is a boost if you choose it to be.

Oh Todd!

*On a funny note. My spinster sisters Anne & Ruth sat me down one summer day and told me about our nephew and that he is gay. They told me I had to accept it.

Why do I have to accept it?

That was my question, I didn't really have any concerns with it. That really should have been it. But, I had to ask. "Does he have a boyfriend?"

Oh Todd!

"You know, someone to smooch with on the couch." Oh Todd "And to kiss goodnight at the door."

Oh Todd!

"Well, what did you think? That he was going to just be gay in his room every night by himself because if that is the case, then we are all gay from twelve on....."

Oh Todd!

"Listen girls, it happened to me once. I was sure I was gay but the fella I was waltzing with told me I wasn't....."

Oh Todd!

Is it any wonder my family shakes their heads where I am concerned?

Faith

I am not saying my family is prudish but talking about some things growing up was definitely off limits. Being gay was one of them. When my mother was growing up there were no gay people. "But Mom, what about Mary, the delivery lady with the brush cut and the wallet with the chain?" oh she said that's just Mary!

"No Mom, that's Joseph!"

To our mother, and those like her, that stuff didn't exist. Well, that was until Faith left her husband and six kids and moved in with Mary. What a scandal! It's not that our mother was not intelligent because she certainly was that. It was more like the carefully crafted life that was fuelled by the bible and those who preached it, homosexuality on any level was unacceptable.

I knew Faith, I liked her a lot, mostly because she liked me and her treatment of me was always kind and generous. I washed dishes in the same restaurant where Faith was a cook. We had lots of talks. Once I asked her what a 'dyke' was. She said you must've heard that about me. I did but at twelve had no idea what it meant.

She was forthcoming with a story that changed the way I think about any other human being, gay or straight. She said she tried to do things the way you were supposed to. "I met a nice man and married him." Together they had six kids. "He was a good father, a hardworking man and a wonderful husband but deep inside I was not happy. Over the years I became more and more unhappy with myself and the secret I carried inside and one day I sat him down and I talked to him about it. Although we knew it would cause a scandal he told me that if I wanted to go, then go. I did and strangely enough he understood."

"Now we are all happy. Well, maybe not happy but we are accepting of things that are not considered normal. This type of lifestyle was normal for me."

Having said all of this, who are we to tell someone how to live, how to feel, how to grieve and how to love? Times have changed and people have changed and I have no doubt that if our mother was here today, the way she would see things would have changed as well because in the end, love is the most important thing on earth and we are continually searching for it.........isn't love what we live to know.

I wonder what Faith would think today what with the United States following in the footsteps of other countries who allow gays to marry. When this all came to light a few of my followers asked what I thought about it and if I approved.

Here is my reply.

A person who lives in a free country should be able to marry whom they please. That is what contributes to the "free".........and besides why shouldn't they suffer like the rest of us?

Our Mother

Our mother was the type that made the most out of life no matter how little we had or how bad the financial situation was. We really did have nothing. When our father died and left her with a pile of kids to raise, it turned out to be more of a blessing than anything. Well, it has taken me decades to say this so bear with me. You see, each and every one of us in our family was born selfish. We were all self-centered and somehow thought that the world revolved around us. Do all people feel this way? I honestly don't know.

All I know is that when our father died and left us destitute, it was not a pleasant experience. Perhaps staying destitute might be less pleasant. We really were lucky that it was him that died and not her, God, forgive me. I suspect that had he been left in such a predicament his solution might be to bring another mother to take care of us. Pity help that man if he had even tried and pity help that poor woman whoever she is.

If one were to be truly grateful for their blessings then one might say we were lucky that they both didn't die and we would all have been separated or have to go to an orphanage. Or that our house didn't burn to the ground leaving us without food, clothing or shelter. We may have been split up with family or found ourselves in overwhelming circumstances that would certainly leave scars for a lifetime. What did happen was God saw it fit to give us our mother who in this boy's eyes was a Giant of a Woman.

She proved over time that resilience and tenacity can get you through anything. She showed by example that determination and willpower can overtake any problem over time. She led us down a path of hard work and perseverance with the motto: If you want something out of this life like a college education, you will have to get one on your own; I cannot give it to you. If you want a job I can probably get you one but I cannot keep it for you. If you want to do something, I mean really do something, then I expect you to go for it and do what it takes to make it happen. If you fail then I will at least know you have tried. If you succeed, then I will applaud your efforts.

She was not the most organized person in the world, yet she always seemed to know where we were. She was no fashion plate, overweight and unkempt, but to us she was beautiful. She was our mother and that was saying something. She possessed greenish gray eyes that slanted on the side, ivory skin and that prematurely white hair. There in the lines of that face was where each and every one of us belonged. In that heart and on that mind we were the only things that mattered to her. You see she was born alone, had no mother of her own so raising a family and having someplace she belonged was so very important to her. We were important to her.

Our mother was an avid reader and a dreamer. She loved Harlequin Romances, probably because our father was anything but romantic. She loved western novels because in among those pages the men were men and the women were ladies. There within the covers of what she was reading were bits and pieces of life that she gathered through the years and cultivated each and every one of them into who she was.

Our mother came from cursing and swearing Scottish coal miners and yet she never swore, she never cursed and she certainly never took the Lord's name in vain. She knew right from the start where her priorities lie. Having her head on straight and having an education when so many in a coal mining town did not, set her path toward being a successful business woman, a successful opponent in a man's world and a successful woman, a maverick.

So, within the walls of our home there was a fiery sense of drive that would not allow our mother to be defeated. She may have been knocked down once or twice but she always got back up again. Those of you who knew my mother know of what I speak, those of you who have never had the pleasure of meeting her, only hearing about her from her children, I am sure can relate on some level...........I hear that there are others just like her out there.

Our mother did not run out and get another man, she didn't need one. She married the only man she would ever love and as a result was happy spending her last years with her true calling and that was in the loving embrace of her children and grandchildren. I said it before, we were all that mattered. She spent a lifetime painting and sculpting young minds into who we are today. So, having said all this, do you think we were really destitute? Hardly!

So there she is Our Mother. She was the original coal miner's daughter. Okay not quite, she came from a long line of them. Raised in a poor coal mining family in Springhill Nova Scotia, she found a place at the table and a place in that family, her father's family. She was born out of wedlock to a woman whose only choice was fight or flight, she flew.

She knew the Gillis clan would take care of the little girl. Raised by a spinster aunt, Vivian learned first-hand just how difficult life was for her coal mining uncles, their friends and neighbours too. The town was built on the principle that the rich coal beds that lie far beneath the earth would provide food and shelter for these hardworking and (in her eyes) valiant men.

If you were never told how old you are and if ages as we know it was never introduced to you, how old do you think you would be? Think about it! I think some days I would be about eighty years old when I try to get out of bed in the morning. But, if I am enthusiastic about the day's events, I might appear to be about fifteen years old. At work where I am at the top of my game, I am about twenty-five years old. When I am with friends and family, intellectually, I am about forty years old. At night I am slightly close to eighty again so therefore slumber appeals to me.

Age really is a state of mind! Ask Betty White.

And what if You were a Potato?

In grade five I was most interested in writing and spelling, music and earth science. They peaked my interest. I often gazed up at the sky wondering if there was any other kind of life out there. In school staying focused was a daily challenge. I was not ADHD or anything like that, I was simply bored. I could easily grasp the assigned work and do it quickly, often completing it before anyone else and then, in the words of my teacher, proceed to talk! This usually disrupted the rest of the class.

The teacher had no clue on how to channel anyone like me. It never occurred to anyone to upgrade me academically or to find some challenging problems for me to solve. I was simply and sternly warned to keep quiet, or else. Not an easy thing for me to do when I possessed such an active mind. At home my mother, upon reports from the teacher, would quite often threaten me with in an inch of my life not to mess up in school.

Since we were a large family our mother tended to buy things in bulk when she could afford it. Potatoes were a staple at our table for every supper meal. So she would buy fifty pound bags of them and keep them in a potato bin in the coolness of the basement. One of us had to retrieve as many potatoes from the bin as a kid could carry. I used the belly of my tee shirt as a potato holder. During one excursion, a potato slipped from my grip and rolled underneath the oil barrel. Out of sight but not out of mind. Of course the one that got away was the one that bothered me. However, I marched forward leaving that potato to die a sad and lonely death in the darkness under the oil barrel.

A few weeks later I again was the designated potato boy and as I was filling the front of my shirt I heard a faint and soft swishing noise. I did not recognize the sound but assumed it was anything from a rebel mouse to a kid playing outside our cellar window. Off I went upstairs with my load of spuds. Mother sent me down again for another load as we were having company. This time the swishing sound was louder than ever. Looking around for clues I could not see anything out of the ordinary until I caught a glimpse of it out the corner of my eye. At first I thought it was a snake but upon viewing the varmint closer I was able to see for myself exactly what it was. It seems that the lost potato was thirsty for water and light so it grew an *eye* some six feet tall so it could retrieve as much sustenance from the sun that shone in our basement window.

I had never seen anything like it. On the cold cement floor under the oil tank was a dehydrated and wrinkled potato and stemming from it was a six and a half foot extension fighting for it's very existence. The swishing noise was the sound it made rubbing against the tank as it crawled toward the light. I told my mother about it and showed her. She told me to show my science teacher at school.

So I ask you, if that potato, something I assumed has lifeless, was willing to fight to survive against all odds, can't I, can't you?

Mother Nature never ceases to amaze me.

I Have Anger Issues

No matter how much therapy I have received, and no matter how much encouragement, love and support, I am still angry. After all I have been through I might very well be a raging alcoholic or a substance abuser, instead I deal with my hurt with anger outbursts. You'll see it the most at work because honestly my coworkers frustrate the hell out of me.

Don't get me wrong, I work with some fantastic individuals and I have formed some friendships that I hope will last a lifetime. I believe it is because I am a good friend. I am honest and forthright, I say sensible things and I try very hard not to judge if you get your personal life in turmoil. Really though, you should try to leave it at the door.

I am also what is known as a good neighbor at work. If your section is dirty, I will help clean it up. If you are overwhelmed, I will help settle you down and all I ask that you give me the same courtesy.

When I come to work I am prepared to do just that, work! I do not bring my phone with me, I do not get personal phone calls and if I do it surprises one and all. I do not bring my personal life to work but then again I am larger than life so some does creep in. I believe that I am a team player always ready to jump in where needed I will work until I feel that I have successfully completed a good job. Okay, I am not perfect but I am pretty good at what I do, just ask the customers.

I have trouble taking criticism. My coworkers might tell you I am moody (well I can on occasion, be a hateful miserable bastard) or they might tell you I am mean (I can also be vindictive, verbally abusive and spiteful) but in my own defense, if I show a little agitation, do not ask me if I am okay, how about you leave me be and I will eventually work it all out in my mind. I will calm down. Just be grateful that I have not taken it upon myself to kill anyone yet ....so that's good right?

I can do my job and I feel that I can do it well but if the others do not do their part it hampers my production. So people Haul Ass! I mean it. I sometimes am the opener or the person who sets up the day for myself and the other servers. If I do my job properly there is adequate enough of everything to have a successful money making day.

However, if you use it, replace it. If it is empty, fill it. If it is not there, inquire. Simple eh? Well everybody doesn't get it so sometimes we are left scrambling to make up for the others who are lacking the same work ethic that I have in place. Fast food outlets tell you to put things back when you are done with them and put them in the correct place. *"A place for everything and everything in its place".* Man what powerful words, not just in the workplace but in life itself.

"Take care of the customer and they will take care of you" I truly believe this and I have built a career on it. I am a firm believer that a business can run without staff but it cannot run without customers. So every time that door opens and customers come in, remember the following. Those people are paying your wages which puts a roof over your head, clothes on your back and food in your belly. And don't ever forget it either. So smile, do your best. Serve hot fresh food in a clean friendly environment and guess what? The rest will take care of itself. So for all of you out there who don't get that, if you are going to work on my shift you had better haul ass.

Jackie McKeown once coined a phrase that I have adopted for a lifetime *"A good server can make up for bad food but good food cannot make up for bad service."* Truer words have never been spoken in the food business. Treat the customers like your job depends on it because guess what, it does. Alienate the public and you will find yourself in an empty dining room.

So where does my anger issues come from?, Incompetence. I absolutely cannot tolerate a few things and they piss me off. Are you ready? Don't tell me how to do my job. Unless you are better at my job than I am do not tell me what to do. Instead watch and learn.

Don't interfere with my tables, in fact why don't you stay away from them. I think I am a pretty capable guy and I can probably handle them just fine. Now on the other hand, If I need help, I will ask.

If left to my own devices I really can accomplish a lot. So why pester me by asking stupid questions? Really people, do your own job and let me do mine.

Let's make one thing perfectly clear, I am here to work! I am never late and I rarely call in sick. If I do arrive early and I do start working (off the clock) do not criticize me. It helps us all in the long run and it adds to the smooth running of our finely oiled machine. No matter how busy we are I can keep up no matter what my age, financial situation, personal status or life in general happens to be embalming me. Never assume that I will run out of steam, I never do. I do however run out of patience. After a shift of listening to the whining of certain staff members, I find myself on the edge of my nerves, add the fact that there has been no follow up to duties and I am left in a predicament, makes me look at you who may very well be texting during your shift, sharing stories of last night's antics or just plain talking, talking, talking. There is work to be done people so let's haul ass and get it done. That makes me happy, it really does.

I was told that on long shifts I get grouchy because I can no longer handle it and to that I ask the following "Are the customers complaining? Nope? the managers? Ha, then I guess that is the problem, somebody isn't hauling ass. I can be just as grouchy on a short shift if things are not the way they should be.

But, I will make you a deal. I will continue to give fast and friendly service with an enormous amount of humility, manners and courtesy where the customers are concerned and therefore all parties will make money. I believe that if you take care of the customers they will take care of you. Please correct me if I am wrong.

*And now the truth, I can blame everyone else for my problems but there is no one to blame but me. I am such a failure when I think about my marriage break up. I let the best thing I ever had slip through my fingers and into the hands of some other man. I was too busy working or chasing after foolish dreams when I should have been chasing her.

I should have quit that job at school years ago. Why did it have to take a life-changing scandal to get me out the door? I hated dealing with an administration that I did not respect and even more performing a mundane routine daily. There was an upside, being a lunch supervisor was very rewarding. I got to see different sides of people. But over all, I was done years ago.

I am missing my music room, the one my wife designed for me. In fact it was probably the only room in which I felt that I could truly be myself. I do expect that one day I will get back to being me and honestly, I am getting there.

I am sorry for any embarrassment that my friends and family suffered and any worry I brought about in living my life in the public eye. I love you all and I appreciate every single one of you. That is really what makes life so wonderful, the moments shared with friends and family that love you no matter what.

Having said all of this, Every day I pick myself up, dust myself off and I keep marching, knowing in my heart that life doesn't have to be perfect to be wonderful.

Keep marching Canton, one doesn't know what's on the other side of the fence until we look.

Angus Gillis:

A Coal Miner's Story
November 1, 1956. Springhill, Nova Scotia.

After supper, on a Thursday afternoon, like every other afternoon, seven year old Vivian Gillis stood on the doorstep of her friend's home breathing in the fresh Nova Scotia air. Despite fall approaching it was a lovelier than usual day, warm and beautiful. Like every other day she would wait for her friend Dorothy to put on her coat and the two of them would go outside to play. Just as Dorothy opened the door to greet her young friend, Vivian felt an unusual rumbling beneath her feet.

For a second or two she felt almost weightless as the compression beneath the earth made its way to the surface. Feeling this turbulence beneath her, Vivian instinctively knew something was wrong. Exactly what was occurring she did not know? Looking toward the mines just a few houses away she could not believe what she saw. What appeared like a mushroom cloud at the mouth of the mine, the smoke and steam rose quickly and brilliantly, almost knocking the girls to the ground. Standing at her kitchen window looking out, Vivian's mother Nora felt the same tremor her daughter did. Knowing full well the damage of a mine collapse or a bump can do her first thought was with her little girl.

The whole event was surreal to the young blonde girl. Hearing her name being hollered, she turned to see her panicked mother running toward her, seconds after the explosion in the mine that turned Springhill nearly upside down. Frozen with fear, the little girl just stood motionless waiting for her mother to rescue her. As Nora Gillis made her way through the falling debris, burning pieces of tin were crashing to the ground all around her.

Taking the girl by the hand, she told her to hurry and the two of them ran down the road together. Nora knew there would be safety at her own mother's house. By this time everyone had filtered out into the street. Most of them were unsure of what had happened but a few men, especially those whose lives revolved around the mine, knew this meant serious trouble.

As the dense smell of smoke and ash filled the air, the picturesque town of Springhill was engulfed in a nasty blanket of toxic and lethal gas. Mothers rushed their children inside as the sirens were screaming loudly around them. Men were running down the street toward the mines to see who was alive and who was not. Immediately some miners emerged from within the smoke and debris and gave word that the boom came from collier #4. Men were dead and dying. The people of Springhill came together as one and without a whisper of doubt, began to work to save the men of the deep dark mines.

Never did it occur to young Vivian Gillis that her father might be hurt or killed. He was her hero. Angus Gillis, at 52 years of age should have long retired from the mine but like all of the men at that time, it was his life's work. He set off for work that day just like every other, not realizing that the events that would follow would change his life forever. Dynamite had always made Angus nervous but it was one of many hazards he faced as a coal miner, just like breathing in the coal dust, the dangers involved with the train cars and with the picks and shovels. These were something he accepted in stride.

It is said that when one is directly involved in any kind of an explosion that the whole situation is so surreal that, quite often, their memory is erased. That's exactly what happened to Angus and the men who worked beside him. A warm tingly sensation trickled up his left arm and as he looked down toward his wrist, heard a small puffing sound and saw a bright flash of light. Within seconds, his body was airlifted, almost weightless and he floated head over heels through space. A few more seconds passed and he found himself lying face down in the rubble and dust. Black. Dark. Cold.

There were a few cries for help as Angus shook his head, he could clearly hear them. It became obvious that the mine had collapsed around him, leaving only a 3 foot tall crawl space. For a moment it occurred to him that his own death was near, after all they were as far down as one could go. Trapped in the mine, so many feet below the surface, he literally could not see his hand in front of his face. Was he blinded by the blast? He did not know for sure. This was the kind of darkness that he could only ever imagine. Covered in blood, dry from the dust, and aching and paining in his chest and back, there was little else he could do but lie there and call out to anyone who might hear a pipe with flowing moderately fresh air was his life line.

As a Catholic family, prayer played a big role in their lives, both above and below ground. As Vivian sat beside her mother at St John's Catholic Church praying for the safe return of her father and his friends, Angus's thoughts drifted toward God as well. He thought about the day he got married in 1937 and how he was able to look out into the faces of his family, especially his mother. He thought about his children's baptisms, walking Vivian to Sunday school, and his own parents Dan & Franny Gillis. He knew deep inside that God was even closer to him now more than ever. They all did. That's why the hymns were sung by the remaining miners. Sitting in their own excrement and slowly starving to death, the days crawled by. Would someone save them? Would they ever see the light of day again? Would ever stare into the face of his wife and daughter again? This prison of darkness and silence was his judge now. He remained quiet, exhausted from the whole ordeal, dozing in and out of consciousness. What was thought to a trickle of water on his hand tasted like blood. Life sustaining blood. We will wait.

For a few days Nora and Vivian stayed at Nanny Phalen's. Friends and relatives were constantly coming and going from house to house, dropping of and picking up supplies and thermoses and food for those who were diligently working on the rescue of the broken and beaten miners. Media flooded the town and the world was introduced for the first time to the small town of Springhill, Nova Scotia.

Family, like Angus's sisters Francess Gillis, and Mary Soppa, his niece Vivian Canton, whom he named his baby girl after, fully pregnant and living in Amherst, gathered together at the old homestead, serving and working and praying. Giving up was not an option. No one knew that more than Nora Phalen Gillis, his wife. Never! One must never give up!

Then the news came....

There is an indescribable feeling when a person finally sees the light, literally. Angus Gillis first saw the bright and overwhelming ray of light brought to him by a pick axe cutting through stone. His tears of relief were welcome and embraced by those whose hard work and resilience has paid off. From 6000 feet below the surface to the top was a trip he would never forget.

Reunited with his family when so many of his peers weren't lucky enough to survive, Angus Gillis was truly grateful for all his blessings.

It took a long time to recover from the after effects of the blast. Quite often he would take a walk down by the mines only to return filled with anxiety. The 39 friends and co-workers that died left an indelible mark on him. A changed man where the mines were concerned it took months and months to fully recover, if he ever really did.

The Number 4 Colliery never reopened. The men who lost their jobs were promised work in the Number 2. Some took the jobs and others didn't. Angus went back to work like any decent man would do for his family and he continued working until the Underground Bump of 1958 when it was decided that the mines would permanently close. He might have been one of the ones killed in that Bump had he not worked the opposite shift that day.

Angus Gillis had seen a lot in his life. He grew up during the First World War, suffered though the Depression, and fought in the Second World War leaving behind a wife and small son. He said goodbye to his parents, lost brothers to the ravages of the coal mining life and yet there still seemed so much to be grateful for.

Of all the things that young Vivian knew there was something she realized during this tragic time that perhaps she never fully understood, and that is the true meaning of resilience and tenacity. It did not take her long to see that she was a part of a very big picture. Her family, especially the women played just as big a role in the coal mining industry as the men did. They all stood to lose as much as the men did. As she stood alongside these fascinating women she soon realized that she was one of them as well. Vivian watched the town, her town come together in a time of tragedy and despair, and how proud it made her feel inside.

Coal Mining in Nova Scotia, a hard old life. It took its toll on so many families, those above and below ground. In 1964 Angus Gillis, like so many other valiant and courageous men of the deep mines said goodbye to his loving Nora, son Sam and a young Vivian Gillis whose was his very heart and soul. Angus Gillis (1906-1964)

Todd Canton & Vivian Gogan

An Interview with Santa

Hosting my own television show for eighteen months was an experience that I will never forget. I was thrilled after I was interviewed on a local station for my friendly obsession with singer Anne Murray for the fact that it led to filming a television special or two and eventually my own half hour talk show entitled *In Conversation with Todd Canton. Of course it would have been a dream come true to interview Anne Murray but when a show is filmed in the basement of the television studio itself, you take what you get. I met a lot of interesting individuals and all in all it was nice. Once in a while we would do a remote interview.*

I have done quite a few interviews. One of the simplest ones I have done has turned out to be one of the most inspiring. I got to interview Santa Claus. All I ever knew about Santa was *A Visit by Saint Nicholas* by Clement C. Moore, *Yes Virginia, There is a Santa Claus* and the Coca Cola ads from which I was told commercialized Santa.

It was just as the annual Christmas parade was coming together that I had Santa slip to the side for a few quick questions. There he stood in a redder than usual suit with a pure white beard, really shiny black boots and a belt that was obviously too big for him. What was also obvious was the fact that this was all for show.

To his side was an elderly gentleman gently caring for Santa, dusting his shoulders, making sure the suit wasn't dirty, the boots not scoffed, and that all was right in the world for Santa, so that he could dazzle the hoards of kids lining the snow covered streets, awaiting his arrival. Cool?

I asked Santa the usual questions and in a minute or two the interview was over and I was on my way to my next conquest.

As I was packing up to leave I spotted the old gentleman kindly smiling at me. He had an indescribable charm about him that made me stop for a moment and talk with him.....

I took the opportunity to ask him a question or two, stating with, "How did you get the privilege of being Santa's helper?"

"Well" he said, "many years ago I was the man that wore that suit and I rode on the sled. I could never quite give up the role. I genuinely enjoyed the shiny faces of the kids who came out in the cold to see me."

"Very nice!" I was quick to say.

"So old timer, then you know the true meaning of Christmas?". I shot toward him.

"I think I do" he quipped with a smile. "You see, I am not just advanced in years as much as I am advanced in wisdom."

"Well said!" I proclaimed remembering something my grandfather always said: **Live and learn otherwise it's not living.......**

"So then, how do you feel about all the commercialization where Christmas is concerned?"

Without blinking, he was quick to state "It has it's advantages as well as it's disadvantages." I couldn't help but chuckle at the truth in his words. It brings people out in throngs doesn't it and they are spending money, that means jobs, you get it right?" "So then the Santa we all know from the Coca Cola ads that you got some fame and fortune as a result of the exposure?"

"Yes, of course and it didn't hurt Coke's business either!" he quipped.

"Oh," I said chuckling "I get it! It has to do with give and take like all business, right?"

"Not quite, it has more to do with communication, reaching out to the people through whatever medium that's the handiest."

"So you are saying that Coca Cola didn't make you famous?"

"Not at all son, Legend has made me famous; I just used them to promote the love and warmth of Christmas. It must've worked too because people are still searching for posters, calendars and all kinds of remnants from that era and that was over sixty years ago. They tend to reach back to happier times in their lives, haven't you?"

"So then where does one go from here?" I inquired.

"We all long for world peace, for hope for the future and for a safer world to live in, correct?"

"Yes Sir" "well you won't find that in a bottle of Coke but you might find it in the spirit of Santa!"

"Santa Claus has been a representative of love and hope and peace for centuries and I promise not to go away now, just when I am needed the most."

"But Santa, it seems like such a greedy and unappreciative world today" "Don't you feel like giving up?"

"Not at all Son, I am inspired by the world around me. I learn from those who have suffered tragedy and yet don't give up. I am inspired by an elephant in India who with three legs walks along with his herd to the watering hole, quite often being helped along by the others in the group. I am inspired by the singing miner from Springhill who when facing his death in the darkness of a mine collapse found comfort singing hymns, and the woman who risked her own life to save a fawn that fell off a bridge into the raging waters and countless others who continue to show courage and that has inspired me."

"It seems to me that nobody shows the true spirit of Christmas, like where is God in all this?" I wondered.

"Look closely and you will see love and where there is love, there is God. He will never abandon you either. After all, it's not about the toys as much as it's the anticipation of them. "It's not about the family gatherings as much as it is the families, and it's not about whose right or who's wrong as long as one is willing to admit that we are all wrong once in a while.

It's about stopping for a moment and appreciating the world around you. About honoring those that have gone on before us and to appreciate those who are up and coming. We can learn from both you know."

"It's about forgiving ourselves and those we have wronged, it's about pride, friendship and humanity and sharing that love and wisdom and tradition with those around us."

"My advice to man today is to learn to accept the beauty in this world that has never faded despite wars, weather and loss of faith in the man above. I know it's all still in there, it just has to be brought to the surface."

"I have to admit, Santa, you have certainly given me something to think about". I said giving my head a shake.

"Well, then I guess I have done my job then haven't I?" Again smiling and winking.

Suddenly, looking into his smiling face, I was able to see the ageless beauty of Santa, the wonders he has performed over the centuries and was reminded as to just how much we loved him and how willing we all were to be good boys and girls so that he might not pass us by. Perhaps I just needed a reminder to place a little goodness back into my heart in this holiday season.

As I walked toward my car I couldn't help but look over my shoulder at him, working away, behind the scenes so that man on the sleigh in the parade could have all the glory and again I was reminded of the real selflessness needed to bring forward the true meaning of Christmas.

If I Had Kids!

I do not have any kids of my own. I however consider some people family. My god-daughter Sara is like a real daughter to me. She is not my only godchild but she is my only godchild in our very large family so there is a spiritual bond between us but hers and my relationship over the years has definitely like that of father and daughter. She is a marvelous person, a hard working woman, a wife and a fantastic mother. She and I both love KFC and we share a similar sense of humor. Since the day she was born we have had a very special relationship. I am so proud of her and the woman she has become.

Spencer is what I envisioned as a son. He is clumsy and awkward but at the same time insightful and interesting. Although he is lost at times I am confident he will find his way. I do look forward to the day he makes me a *grandfather* and he can see a smaller version of himself to deal with. I am chuckling to myself at the very thought.

These of course are fantasies that I and I alone have created. It is to fill an empty void in my life that should have been filled with children of my own. True. The fact is these people have parents and I am quite sure that there is no room for me in the middle of these busy lives. Still, here I am loving and caring from across the room and in his case, across the country.

My wife told me the reason she did not want kids was because she felt she had no maternal instincts. Not that she would ever get the chance to find out as she wouldn't be given the opportunity to hold the baby as it would be mine from day one. If you have trouble believing that, ask the dog. And that child would no doubt weigh about 400 lbs because it would at least eat like I do and if he or she did not possess my hollow leg. I am lucky that with my over charged appetite that I'm as slim as I am.

I also think that with Sherry's shyness and my outward personality, you might start out with a quiet angel and once you got it going would have to spend the rest of the day trying to shut it up. However, I am sure he or she would possess a grand sense of humor, a kind heart for animals and musical knowledge like nobody else s.

Now here is one for you. I would not be a good father. Enter: Alfonso. He is my fantasy child. He is also my conscience. He would not get out the door for school in the morning without at least a half a glass of orange juice, a scrambled egg and a slice of toast. I think that is so important to keep his active mind and body alive. Sensible meals and a sensible life for my Alfonso. In bed at a decent time every evening and up early in the morning. With his high IQ I would constantly be on guard with any questions he might throw my way but also just in case he planned on having me exterminated, that nasty eight year old..

I know that he would not like how I handle bullies, by hiding behind trees and following him as he makes his way through life. I would simply tell him that I love him more than life itself and that all my smothering is because of that love. He would be driven (by me) everywhere he had to go. My Alfonso would only attend a private school because as you know he is very special. By the time he is thirty and dateless I would simply allow him to continue to live in my basement so that he won't be exposed to any diseases that might take his life. He would not be allowed to smoke or drink but once in a while we would go to my family home for a meal so that they could see the progress I have made with my little Alfonso. What a life!

Got a problem with that?

The Long Walk Home

When my dog Rozie was recovering from illness and a series of procedures it became apparent early on that exercise was a must. A dog needs to walk. In many ways it is their job. In doing so they get fresh air and sun. It is not only good for their well being it is good for ours as well. I can see that the walk makes her feel good and when she feels good, so do I.

We venture out every morning no matter what the weather. Although some days the weather is discouraging, we venture forward anyway. Honestly, we venture forward despite any odds, simply because giving up on each other is not an option.

The best part of the walks is this is *our* time and even though it lasts a short time, it continues to keep our bond active. Fourteen years is a long time for any two people to love each other but when it is Daddy and dog it is so much more deeper.

So out we go.

I hope for 500 yards a day and most days we make it but some days we cut it short. The farther we go the longer the walk home. Of all the journeys I take and have taken it is the long walk home with my girl that means the most to me......

we are home, time for a nap.

In Honoring my Mother!

If I were to ascend the stage to accept an Oscar as Best Actor, I would certainly thank all my friends and family. Then, of course, the members of the Academy. I might then send thanks to my Director, Producer and my fellow cast mates for putting up with me, but it really would not mean a thing if I did not at least acknowledge my parents and especially my mother, Vivian Canton.

Now over the years I have written everything that could be said about that woman so if I were to single her out on this auspicious occasion then I might very well say:

It was upon the rude awakening of my father's death that I really took notice of my mother. There she stood at forty-three years of age, overweight and slovenly. Whatever was going on with her personally was overshadowed by the fact that her husband was dead, she had a pile of children to raise and financially strapped future faced us all.

Ladies and Gentlemen, that woman went without so that we, her children might have, and because of all of that, are humble people and smile at the mention of her name. This Oscar belongs to her because you don't know this until now but she was the star of our family and we are the jewels that dangle from her.

If I am willing to pass up the glory of this very special moment to shine the light on our mother then I ask you this. Since she is everything I have ever said about her and then some, is it any wonder that we all miss her so much today?

In honoring my mother I would certainly remember that twinkle in her eye, the sultry sound of her voice, her sharp wit and keen sense of humor and her, our mother. Ladies and Gentlemen, a sincere thank you for listening.....(I am sure by this time although the audience might be mesmerized, the music would have drowned me out) Mother, you were the star of our family.

A Message to Michael!

When my friend Michael became a father, I made the remark that this kid was a gift from God. Michael, whose childhood was less than perfect, is a non-believer. In his world, God does not exist! He has adamantly stated this on many occasions but you cannot shake my faith, I am a believer.

"Prove that God exists if you can" he often challenges. So here is my response. Back in the day when my father passed away I could not understand why. I was eleven years old. But as time went on I was able to see it for myself. Had things been different and HE had taken her and not him, it would have likely been our father's only recourse to find us another mother. Well, pity help that poor woman whoever she might be.

What HE did do was give us our mother (who was in this boy's eyes a giant of a woman) and she showed us the way. Now having said that I thank God every day for HIS having given us our mother.

To you Michael, I say, considering all the obstacles one has to face in this world, it is more than likely that one day you will sit in a lonely hospital hallway with your head in your hands with worry and I am quite sure that it will not be my mother's name you call out, but rather God's name.

Don't worry Michael, I will be praying too, I have it in good with HIM.

PS.... If I never said so, I am proud of you. Every time I see you with your boy and the way you are with him makes me love you more.

Every once in a while we need to be reminded about the sunshine in our lives and just who is sending it down to us.

She Loves Me Not!

It is never easy when a marriage ends so when I tell you that it really wasn't easy for me would you get it? I am so much of a public person and that is one thing. The other being that I am the type of person who lets very few into my personal life. My intensely private personal life.

Enter Sherry. I met that lovely quiet girl when she was fourteen years old and I was sixteen and a half. It was those blue eyes that I fell in love with and I was invited beyond those eyes into a world filled with love and laughter, food, music and emotion. I loved her and she loved me!

Since I grew up with a domineering mother and many opinionated sisters it was only fitting that I marry someone so shy and reserved. And marry her I did on a sunny Saturday afternoon in the same church my parents did some forty years before. The ceremony was predictable and the banquet divine. The dance was rowdy and so were the people. We had come a long way to stand there in front of family and friends to become one.

A few months later we moved from our home town to start a life together. Just us.

We led a quiet life, socialized a little and happy to do so because Sherry was a fantastic cook and I the perfect host. All in all it was a nice life. But then the socializing began to diminish. After a while no one was invited over. Ours was a quiet house. She became reclusive and quiet. Too quiet for someone like me who was bursting at the seems.

I felt a little stifled and closed in, she did not. My group of friends were never hers and she kept pretty much to herself working away diligently at a career that would take her to new heights.

I was the dreamer of the group searching for fame and fortune in TV and in writing books. I found some. Fame yes, fortune no. The spotlight always seemed to be on me and as far as I know with her, that was okay as she shied away from such things.

Somewhere along the way we lost each other. She was hard to read at the best of times and so if the signs were there I did not see them or I wouldn't let myself see them. I was working a lot and she was left alone a lot. Then she got sick. Her back had already bothered her but what happened this time crippled her. It was suggested that she join a gym to strengthen her back muscles. It worked. It strengthened her mind as well. She began to come out of her shell and got in with a group of friends that I was not introduced to. I began to see the changes in her but passed it off to her getting older, her mother's passing and her.

What I didn't know was that in her own quiet way she was taking inventory of her life and wanted change. She loved me once, now, she loves me not! Or so she says. We are apart, I still wear the ring and who knows how the two of us will fare apart. You will never see in print or hear me ever say a bad word about that woman. Once thing is for sure. I will never love anyone like I love her, not just today, ever.

So where do we go from here? Well, there is no more *we* so it is up to me to march forward and I can honestly say I do not know what the future holds. Do you?

I am not alone, I am on my own. I found out through my scandal that I am stronger than I ever thought I was and it has made me more determined than ever to succeed. After all of this I can't give up now.

However, every once in a while I am reminded of what a loser I really am for letting that wonderful girl down by allowing us to grow apart. My only hope is that she finds the happiness she so richly deserves.

She doesn't like it when I write about her but if I am able to convey any thoughts on love then how could she not come to mind. Never mind Anne Murray, India von halkien, and even Rozie, Sherry, you are without a doubt, the love of my life.

Applause Please!

Despite any warnings by the weather man to stay inside, I found my way to the store. On the way home in the freezing rain, I slipped and fell spilling my groceries and in an attempt to collect myself continues down the slippery slope of life. I did make it home and despite the fact that I was soaked to the skin, I survived. Don't believe me? just ask my neighbor to see the video she took on her phone.

Applause please.

Well, there was a man from Ontario who was able to get his hands on the lambskin paper that Canadian currency is printed on. He went to Xerox and had placed in his office at work, the best of the best laser copier and printer. Not an ostentatious sort he quietly ran off sheets of twenties. Didn't draw much attention to himself in any lavish way and over the next two years was able to run off about $225, 000 in these crisp bills. Now, the question is, How did he get caught?

Well, it seems with all he did use the money for, he didn't make the payments on the Xerox and low and behold, they repossessed it. In an inspection of the machine, they found a sheet of bills. True story! Lesson: if you have a goose that's laying golden eggs, take care of it. Applause please!

Here's another one. At high school near our town it was fast becoming the trend for young girls to apply their lipstick and kiss the bathroom mirrors causing frustration and more work for the janitors. So, an intelligent teacher took it upon themselves to educate the ladies by taking several small groups of them into the washroom along with the janitor, to show them how difficult they were making life for some people. The teacher instructed the janitor to remove the smeared lipstick. He did so by approaching his cart and retrieving his toilet brush and bucket. He then gave the mirror a few swipes with it. Afterward he took some paper towel and attempted to wipe it off. The girls looked on in horror and I guess that problem was solved once and for all. Applause please!

Friends: Don't Let the Good Times Pass You By!

I am a firm believer that a little patience and understanding can get you though any thing. Unfortunately most days, all I have is a little patience and understanding. But I do have friends. They come in all shapes and sizes, and differ on just about every level including color, sex, age and community standing. They make me who I am today and they allow me to be all that I can be without knocking me down and then kicking me while I am down.

I really am a lucky man and if I ever had the privilege of walking across the stage to accept a Grammy I would certainly have a few people to thank. But honestly, the first one would be me. I am the one who gets me out of bed every morning, cleans and dresses me and marches me out the door. It is out there that I have a huge circle of friends. This has come about because I am once and for all, a friend first.

While I have expressed that I think of Spencer as a son and Derek as my brother the truth is I am their friend and they are mine. Jeremy Lepine means and awful lot to me as does so many others, Nora Plourde for one, with her sense of humor, caring heart and her unwavering loyalty to me. For these people and so many more, I am truly grateful and even more a truly blessed man.

The ones that mean the most to me were there when I needed them during the most emotionally challenging time of my life. For that I will forever be indebted to them. Even if they are not standing here in front of me at this very moment, they were there when I needed them and that moment in time has left an indelible mark on my heart. Same as those who felt it best to abandon me or to show their true colours when the chips were down. I promise to never forget you either!

Friends are like favorite songs, they come and go. Some become the soundtrack of your life, others are simply moments in time. I used to think the song Wake me up before you Go-Go by WHAM was the ultimate dance song, well after Stayin' Alive by the Bee Gees, Hot Stuff by Donna Summer and All About the Bass by Meghan Trainor and so on...times change, people change and tastes change. Adele's 21 is one of my favorite albums of all time, that and Book of Dreams by the Steve Miller Band, She's So Unusual by Cyndi Lauper, Band on the Run by Wings, Woman in Love by Barbra Streisand and Rumors by Fleetwood Mac. Then there are one hit wonders and we are the ones left wondering as their voices are some of the nicest on earth. Like their music some singers come and go, just like friends.

Some things don't change however. I miss the spectacular voices of Karen Carpenter, Lesley Gore, Patsy Cline and Nat King Cole. I believe that all of them would still be singing today much to my ears and soul's delight. I consider Barry White to be the best male voice on earth, okay Elton John and Billy Joel too!

I think Barbra Streisand is the best singer in the world but Celine can give her a run for her money. I think Josh Grobin is spectacular but so was Michael Jackson in the spiritual sense. I love Shania Twain and adore Carrie Underwood. kd lang has a spectacular range as does Sam Smith and I absolutely love Adele. So, basically saying that music can make or break the mood, enhance the evening, or wake you up to the world as we know it.

Friends do come and go but it is truly a great feeling when you have a list of people that you can call any day or night and they are there for you. Not everyone can say the same.

I think it is quite remarkable that I could make a comparison between two things and one of them not being food

The Dark Dogs of Depression

Depression is something I have battled my whole life. I never suffered from the debilitating kind rather the menacing type that crawls into your dreams at night, affects your energy level during the day, and even upsets your food intake and digestive processes. *It affected my self-worth and kept me, on occasion, from being all I can be. It is another cancer.*

As this cancer grew and spread rapidly..........

Since I was facing a personal scandal head on, I really did not have anywhere to turn. I attended regular therapy sessions with a gentle soft spoken woman but I was unable to focus. In my mind I had done nothing wrong and yet, in my gut I knew I was the person that put me in this position. Self-doubt was creeping into my thoughts during my rest periods and during my wide awake ones. Everyone wanted to talk to me about what was going on. Most I felt were looking for a story. What kept me going was the fact that those who believed in me continued to treat me the same way they always had. I felt unworthy of such loyalty and devotion and yet, there it was.

As low as I allowed myself to feel and as down as a man can get, thoughts of my father's demise all those years ago crept into my thoughts. I was feeling all those feelings again, betrayal, abandonment and in some ways cowardice. How dare you die! Why didn't you fight to live? How could you leave me, us? It was like when he was told that he had cancer, he laid down and died. I knew that I did not want to die. Giving up meant dying and I absolutely did not want that. There had to be more to life than this. I knew inside that I was a good man, my mother made sure of it. I had to keep marching.

In the references made by my mother about her father being a coal miner who faced uncertainty and possible death by going underground, still he had a family to feed. Then there was her, a widow at 43 with a houseful of children to feed and she didn't give up. So then you have me facing, in some ways, a bigger cancer than theirs and yet giving up is really not an option. I looked in the mirror and although I didn't hate what I saw, I didn't like it all that much either.

But more than all of that, I looked into my little dog's face. There in the gentle eyes of my girl, I could see love. Not a romantic kind, a true love. She was after all, my wife's dog. I never wanted one. Too much responsibility I thought. Yet in the first forty-eight hours after we met each other, the dog decided that I was more than okay. It has never wavered. So when I look at her and see how much she needs me it makes me want to do better. She makes me want to be a better man. In God's eyes I want to do right by her. I want someday to go to heaven one day and see my parents and in doing so I want to have a clear conscience. I want to leave this earth knowing I helped it to be a better place and that I have treated the human race, the animal kingdom and the earth itself in a respectful manner. I have always nurtured and acknowledged children and old people and have never hurt anyone intentionally. Never.

Any self-doubt was fading, albeit slowly and I was feeling a little better. Instead of laying around and feeling sorry for myself, I made myself get out of bed and go to work. I put on my face every day much in the same way a woman puts on her makeup. I had a professional brave face. Actually, it was more like a whole suit of armor. It protects me. I did my job generically and went through the motions. I had to because my little girl depended on me. She sat like an angel and waited for me every single day, greeted me like I had just come back from the war and it made me want to do better. I had to do better! It was fueled by the love I felt. How could I not want to do better knowing and feeling all the love that was coming my way. Not just from her but from all those who reached out to me especially my family and friends.

I did have a few personal friends that I could rely on to take my mind off of things if only for a moment. Derek, someone half my age has the wisdom of someone twice that. He has truly been a constant source of inspiration *He insinuated his way beyond the shield and into my very personal and private world. That boy would check on me every day and show up at the oddest hours to make sure I was doing alright. I insisted that I was doing fine. I was not comfortable sharing personal details with anyone so I felt it best if I put the run to him and all his good intentions. Still, he continued to show up day after day.*

You have to remember that when someone is as private and as intense as I am, it is not easy to penetrate my very solid walls. After all I was the 'go to' guy. I was the one who everyone called for advice; the one who people leaned on for moral support and was always the sensible voice of reason. I never ask anyone for help. Everyone assumed that I was as strong as I appeared. Instead, I was seriously, a beaten and broken man.

I felt that my emotions fueled by self-pity were running at full tilt, and that they might be too much for someone so young to handle so I started to put things in perspective. Why not get out of bed and cook that boy something to eat? In fact, why not clean up your house and in doing so clean up your act. Also, this feeling sorry for yourself is getting you nowhere Canton. These were not Derek's words, they were mine. He didn't have to say anything. He simply referred to me as his brother and told me every day that he loved me.

I could accept no praise. I did not want to hear what a great man I was nor did I deserve such loyalty. I could not for the life of me imagine what I ever did to deserve such devotion. It did occur to me one afternoon that maybe all those times I spoke to God for answers that they were sitting right in front of me in the form of an angel, an angel who loves me, just because......

I didn't know how to thank him. Of course I could make him a cake or maybe give him my car but what does all that mean? I wanted something a little more permanent than that. So I did what I do best, I included him in my writings, I dedicated my book Food For Thought to him stating "This book is dedicated to Derek, thank you for being a friend just when I needed one"

The two of us made a pact for life. If either of us was in a situation that was overtaking us, we make it known that "I need you" not want you, "need you" and we would drop everything and come to the rescue. Over the last couple of years we both have exercised this option, not once taking our love and affection for granted. We really do have something special, a bromance of epic proportion. For that and all my blessings, I am eternally grateful.

The House on Farnham Road

When my wife and I came to an agreement where our separation, our lives and our home was concerned, I had to find a place suitable for Rozie and me to live. You have to remember that I really wasn't myself. I was simply going through the motions but some things were quite clear.

That was *her* house! Sherry was the handyman in our relationship. Being a perfectionist, she insisted on doing things her way. She was the one who manicured the front and back yards. She worked endless hours in the yard in and out of the garden. While I enjoyed the comfort of air-conditioning in my music room, she was content getting in touch with Mother Earth. Many a summer evening was spent around a fire, drinking beer, talking and loving. She hired someone to build an earthen oven. This unusual contraption cranked out some fantastic rustic meals. She even went as far as cooking our Christmas dinner outdoors. It was by far the most favourable of all the meals in memory and simply amazing in its delivery. She has always been a masterful chef but she outdid herself with this one.

Also, with me leaving, I knew that as long as she was in our house she would be safe, that is what really mattered. Besides I had so many other things on my mind.

I found a small apartment that allowed pets in a revamped and aging mansion on Farnham Road. What sold me on it was the access to an immense outdoor patio deck. This would be great for Rozie and for Daddy. We made the best of this situation and together, Daddy and dog, *ventured forward.* During this transition I placed my personal effects in storage and sadly, I lost my home but especially my beautiful music room. I had to downsize my life in many ways while Sherry was building a new and wonderful existence, in short, a life without me.

My passion has always been and hopefully always will be, cooking. At the house on Farnham Road, this was no exception. I drove my in-house neighbours crazy with the daily aromas from my apartment. My specialty was homemade turkey stuffing, hamburger stew, sautéed shrimp on rice and oven baked cakes. You name the flavour, I made them. My best one was a bananas and cream cake with chocolate frosting or my bread pudding with brown sugar sauce. Or was it my double fudge chocolate cake or maybe my peanut butter and banana supreme with cream cheese frosting.

Sorry, got a little carried away.

As unusual as my menu was so were the residents I encountered in the House on Farnham Road. There were people of all shapes and sizes and of all ages. One or two retired people and a couple of twenty-something students who attended a nearby university, and some out-of-towners who required temporary lodging. Most relationships or friendships formed were not long lasting. I tried not to get attached. And then something wonderful happened. And it happened over a set of keys and a poutine.

Jeremy Lepine resided in apartment 8 upstairs in the House on Farnham Road. He worked at one of the fast food places in town and I would often see him coming and going, little else. He traveled by bicycle through all kind of weather and as far as I knew, never really bothered with anyone. Once by mistake he left his keys in the community mailbox. This would certainly make it difficult to get into the building let alone his apartment.

Being the Good Samaritan that I am I called his place of employment and left a message for him to call me. He did and explained that he was visiting family and would subsequently return the following day. I asked him where he would like the keys left. He told me to simply leave them under his mat outside his apartment door. I consciously kept my eye out as he still couldn't get in the building unless someone opened the outside door for him. I just happened to be in the backyard with my dog when he and his mother pulled in the yard. I gave him his keys, he thanked me and I handed a small container to his mother saying simply, "this is for Jeremy, my specialty, it's a poutine." She thanked me and said, "You are kind".

A day later I am home in the middle of my shift to let Rozie out when Jeremy descended the stairs with my empty container in hand. He stood there with an amazing grin on his face and proceeded to tell me that it was one of the best poutines he had ever had. Great, I said, come on in for a minute. (I always made my own gravies by saving the broth produced from whatever I was cooking at the time. Flavor is the key ingredient in anything you cook.) Earlier in the day I had I thrown together one of my homemade stuffing and with it fresh out of the oven, offered him a sample. I swear to God something happened, right then and there. I found a friend. We had little in common, first of all he lived on the computer and knew it inside and out, I did not. He was a gamer and I, a music lover. He watched movie after movie and I found it hard to sit still. He never left his apartment and I hated to stay home. What we did have in common was that we both laughed at the same stupid things and we both have enormous appetites so cooking and eating has become a substantial part of our friendship.

That friendship being one that I feel will last me a lifetime, at least I hope so.

He almost seemed reclusive in his dimly lit apartment that I referred to as "the cave". I insisted that he dine with me downstairs and I included him in all I did be it running an errand or taking a trip to the city. He might tell you that I got him out of a slump but I insist that he was a constant in keeping me from going insane. He was sensible to talk to and he listened intently to anything I shared with him. I told him up front the trouble I was in and offered him an 'out'. He refused. I did ask him to tell his mother my situation as I wanted no surprises. She told him that she trusted his judgment. For all of this I am truly grateful. Over the course of the next year we talked about everything under the sun. He saw me at my best and he saw me at my worst and the guy still came back.

Jeremy is quite a cook himself and I have been the eager recipient of his efforts. He reintroduced me to rice and I must say he gets better every day. Rice was always something that was used as a filler. In fact the only time I enjoyed it was when sweet and sour chicken was stuck to it. Yet when he made his broccoli and mushroom rice it was downright spectacular. Eating has been a great hobby for the both of us. Another specialty is breakfast and I think I do it rather well. Well, Jeremy never complains.

It seems a beautiful young Filipino lady from work had taken a liking to him and I urged him to go for it. He did and now the two of them live together in town and subsequently planned marriage. I worried when he moved out of the House on Farnham Road that we might lose touch but I am happy to say that we have remained the closest of friends. Jeremy, you are a brother to me in my ever expanding chosen family. Since then

Richard Todd Canton

they have married in a simple but beautiful ceremony that reminded my heart that true love continues to exist.

I also met Brenda McGrath and her dog Oreo, and then there's Scott, Tony, Lawna and Mercedes but it is Cody White and Ariana Pinsent who captured my heart for a lifetime.

Thank you all for filling my long days with life, laughter and love.

Still Crazy after all These Years!

There are many words of wisdom that I could pass along but nothing is more important than 'staying true to yourself" Of all the things I have learned and of all the wisdom I have attained I have come to one conclusion. You will die trying to please everyone so concentrate on those that matter.

We spend our lives bending and stretching to please others, how about what makes us happy. Dare to dream and dare to go after those dreams. This has become one of my many *life statements* that I share with the world but not before I apply them to myself. Think about it, what good are words of wisdom if they are not followed by the preacher himself.

Do as I say not as I do was a phrase that help mankind lose hold of a generation. We smoked because our parents did, same with drinking. Take it a step forward and you realize that we learned everything by observing our parents and siblings so after that kind of an education why would be anything but a copy of them. Only to be told not to do as they were doing which left them disgruntled but to do exactly the opposite. What is an impressionable young mind supposed to think?

Therefore I think you stand back and take a look around you, decided what is best for you and run toward it. Otherwise you are not being true to yourself. It really is alright to change paths midstream, just don't get lost. Keep a clear head about yourself and despite any odds, go for it! Expect the worst and hope for the best. Now tell me if the following does not make sense. Take care of your body, it is the best instrument you will ever own. Take it out for a run or a long walk on a sunny day. Feed it good and nutritious food and allow it to get lots of rest. Take care of your body and it will subsequently take care of you.

Either I make a bundle of sense or I really am still crazy after all these years.

Twist of Fate

When my friend Linda's son died in a tragic accident, I was nothing short of heartbroken. I can only imagine how she felt. I knew I had to go and see her, to hug her and tell her how sorry I was for all involved. Instead, because I was so wrapped up in my own troubles that really I didn't have time for her. I spend most days going to work, going home and going to bed.

I just couldn't muster the strength as my depression had worsened over the news of his untimely death. What I knew I would do was wait a suitable time and once all the supportive friends and family left, I would step up. Pretty good idea, eh? But then I thought to myself, does she need a hug today from someone like me who can do so with a true sign of human decency attached.

My friend Lannie called me and invited me to a bonfire. I refused. He refused as well, to take no for an answer. I told him that I really wasn't up to it. His response to that was exactly what I needed to hear. "Canton, you cannot it in the apt by yourself for another day, come and sit with us" I asked if he still lived in the same place and yes he did. I got in my car and drove to the edge of town, followed the old country road all the way out and eventually came to his quiet neighbourhood with just a few homes in a welcoming cluster. The evening sky was particularly beautiful that night and Lannie was right, it was exactly what I needed.

As I sat there taking in all the beauty of the summer evening I took little notice of the neighbourhood or of a lady's silhouette along the fence in the moonlight. Still I felt compelled to take a second look. Linda. What??? I couldn't believe my eyes. She lived next door and I feel God brought me to her in the gentleness of the sultry evening. I found my way over to where she stood, hugged her from over the fence and I believe we both felt the importance of that moment.. I am not sure if it is what she needed but it turned out to be exactly what I needed.

Now things like this have happened to me more times than I can count. It seems that when I don't go where I should, Fate seems to bring it to me.

Life Doesn't have to be Perfect to be Wonderful......

With all the pain and suffering in the world, I really do not have a lot to complain about. Yet I still do. So, every once in a while I force myself to take inventory of my life. In doing so I stack my haves and my have-nots and it becomes quite clear that despite any rough roads that I may have traveled and any bumps and bruises I may have received along the way, it is still a pretty good life.

Is it perfect? Hardly. Is it worth living? You bet!

So here is where I am today. I am still working with my true love serving in the food business. I will work until I can work no more. My days of being Mr Canton, the teacher's assistant are behind me forever. My wife and I sadly are heading for a divorce. I continue to write and to acknowledge and nurture every person I come in arm's length of. I promise to never lose my sense of humor or my quirky way of looking at life. I still have my Rozie who is nearing fifteen years of age and all I can say is I am so proud of her and me..

My family is doing well, amazing really that we are all still alive so many years after Mom & Dad. I continue to reside in Truro on Farham Road and so if you ever find yourself up this way drop by and we'll have a cup of tea or maybe we'll go to lunch at Murphy's, or even take a trip out to the Masstown Market. I promise to introduce you to some very interesting people who reside here.

I could always get behind the wheel and we could head up to Springhill to visit the Anne Murray Centre. Even if you are not a fan of that lady it is still a chance to get to see a Grammy Award up close or a gold or platinum album, she has plenty of those. Marcie Meekins, who runs the place is a welcoming and generous soul (and her mother makes the best Saskatchewan Cake....just sayin').

If you do visit the Maritime Provinces bring your camera so you can capture the essence of the landscape and the spirit of the people who make this part of the world so beautiful. I do warn you, you might not want to leave. Again, thank you to the people of Truro Nova Scotia and to all who have sent their support in the form of phone calls, letters, emails and by word of mouth, I feel the love you've sent my way. It is because of this and so much more that I have come to the conclusion that Life Doesn't have to be Perfect to be Wonderful!

Snowbird

I am quite sure that in 1969 when Gene MacLellan wrote the song Snowbird that he never knew that it would ever become the hit it did and I am quite sure he had no idea the impact that two minute song would have on the career of Anne Murray, the music world and the heart of a lonely fatherless boy. It has become my anthem.

He spoke about having a broken heart because the one he loved forever was untrue and wished only to fly away with the birds to some other world far from one filled with hurt and pain. Me too.

Add a voice like Morna Anne Murray's and you have a song that not only spoke to all Canadians but to the music world. Others liked it too, after all, they bought millions of copies. Even biggies like Elvis and Bing Crosby recorded it.

By now everyone knows my connection to Miss Murray, including her. I thought as a grieving boy that she was singing directly to me to somehow make me feel better and to become more accepting of the death of my father. Now that was forty years ago and that woman's voice still sings to my heart even though she is retired from the business, what a gift she has left each and every one of us with her talent.

Anne emerged from the crowd on Singalong Jubilee, a barefoot girl with a down to earth approach to life and music. It did not take long before the world took notice. Catherine MacKinnon was *the* female star of that show with her rich cosmopolitan voice but never quite made it outside the Maritimes, Her only other competition was Myna Lorrie who was a songwriter as well as a singer, pretty too and yet the hands of fate kept her close to home as well. But not our Anne. Bill Langstroth, the host of that program recognized her talent long before everyone else did and he nurtured it. During the process he fell under her spell and in love which led to their eventual marriage.

Anne's career took her around the world, and has been a respectable one with little or no scandals, the usual ups and downs but one thing never changed with her and that was her sense of self. She remained true to herself and her music delivering to us (and especially me) a pure, rich and sometimes sultry voice that took hold of a song and made it her own. Her natural ability led her toward songs of feelings and love. We all felt the love she was singing about and were able to relate.

At 70, Anne is retired but she still appears yearly at a Centre built in her honour in her hometown of Springhill, Nova Scotia. She meets, greets and interacts with every person that visits her on the anniversary of the home of her gold and platinum records, awards galore and memorabilia that might convert the most defiant of fans. She will sign autographs, pose for photos with fans, share stories and even have a laugh or two.

Gene MacLellan, thank you not only for Snowbird but for the amazing collection of songs that I recognize in the first few notes no matter where I am at the time. Anne, a sincere thank you for so many reasons that even a diligent fan like me could ever list.

My story entitled "the Songs in my Heart" was featured in Canadian Living Magazine in September of 2004

The Songs in my Heart

This is probably the most personal thing that I, Todd Canton, have ever written.

I was eleven years old when my father died.. West Highlands School, grade six, Amherst, Nova Scotia, Canada. His death made such an impact that I am quite sure that forty years later that I am not entirely over it. I remember school at the time because I felt that it was the most important thing in my life. My father's death interrupted my educational process, my personal life and me, the little boy who was left without a father, I was lost.

When you lose someone who sits down at your table there is an emptiness that finds it's way inside of you. That emptiness for me was a strong feeling of despair. So much so that I wished that I could die so that I would not have to endure those feelings any longer. I didn't want to die in the same sense my father did. I just did not want to feel anything anymore. I wanted the world to go away.

As a Catholic it was my first instinct to pray. I prayed to God to let me hear or see a sign of hope.

Since I was unable to sleep at night, I found myself quite often gazing up at the beautiful summer skies. The view from my bedroom window was able to fully capture the vastness of the Tantarmar Marshes. It was then that I knew the truth. In my dreams my father was so near. In my sleep he was where he should be on my mind, in my heart but physically....he was gone. In the quiet beauty of the silent evenings I wished upon star after star that some other kind of life form, an alien life-form or an angel, would land quietly and rescue me from the pain and suffering I endured at such a young age.

I also lived through fantasy, you know the kind, where my father was on a secret mission for the

Canadian government and he had to be dead in order for all of us to be safe. Then one day a helicopter would land in the tall grass near our house and our father would quietly slip into our home and back into our lives, even if it meant he was going to leave on another mission. At least I would see him again. This of course, never came to be.

It was my mother who was able to soothe my aching soul. She was my saving grace, the one who knew me best, although I wonder now if she even realized the positive impact that she made on me. I remember me as a complicated little boy.

My mother bought me a radio for my room and with it came headphones. She was always one to encourage us to get to know the world around us. Many of my sleepless nights were spent listening to All Night Radio from New York or, if the night was clear, just about anywhere in the world. With that small contribution from my mother she opened up a whole new world to me, music. Of course there were lots to choose from but it did not take long for me to gravitate toward those who sang from the heart. It was the voice and the words and the music that picked me up and carried me away.

My room became the sanctuary that I so badly required and music, my medicine.

My father was gone, a harsh reality. I sat in the very chair where he had sat in weeks before, staring at the same screen that we all, as a family, enjoyed, but he was not there. But she was, the nice barefoot girl, sitting in a rocking chair, singing to me, "I'm just sittin' back sittin' here lovin' you."

For a moment I felt better..........

I first realized that the voice that was singing was singing to me when I heard the words "I can't believe that you're honestly thinking of leaving me......." Well now that is exactly what I was wondering..."Until the light says goodbye to the night and your face I see, I'll just keep biding my time while the glow from the wine makes a fool of me......" --- -- If I am a good boy and a good man then one day we will all be together again. There's that Catholicism again. Okay then tell me more......." it's a long distance phone and I feel so alone here without him....(the Call)." Then it was time to put a face to the words. Anne Murray was singing songs, sad songs...."Hard as I try I can't reach him...." I liked her voice and I could relate to the words. Not her words. Those were the very sad words of Gene MacLellan, Anne just made them bearable. So I kept listening and through the singing I found hope. "Put your hand in the hand of the man who stilled the water..." The sadness began to fade...."Got a feeling in my heart, that it's time for us to start to sing.... sing together again"(from Sing High, Sing Low by Brently Titcomb)

It was again through music that I could feel the darkness begin to fade. The worst two years of my life were coming to an end and I, Todd Canton was feeling better. Anne Murray, who was trying to find a place in the music business was making a significant impression in my heart. Her way was my way and I was hooked.

Over the years as I matured so did Anne's music and my attitude toward it. I am happy to say that I slow-danced to You Needed Me at my wedding and all of us have waltzed to and sang along with Could I have this Dance, even if you don't want to admit that you knew the words.

So now when I go to school everyday at junior high, and I look into the faces of those troubled individuals whom I work with, I see bits and pieces of my own life. I use, to the best of my ability, my life's lessons telling them that you really can overcome obstacles in your life, to never give up and that there is always 'hope'. I should know.

Forty years of music and a lifetime of memories that go with each and every tune. I wasn't the only one who thought Anne Murray was singing to them but I bet I was the one who appreciated it the most.

Anne Murray you are responsible for the songs in my heart.

I told you it was personal........

Anne, I begin and end with you.......

Printed in the United States
By Bookmasters